Sometimes you're sad when you finish a book because you want to keep on growing with it. Sometimes the author so gradually gains your trust that, by the end, you welcome her as you might a knowledgeable friend who delights in whispering edifying wisdom in your ear as you walk together through hard questions and challenging truths. Abigail Wallace invites us on a journey we don't know we want to take until we find ourselves on the road with her. As any great work should leave us, I found myself with as many satisfying answers as I did honest questions.

—Kat Silverglate, founder of *The Ridiculous Hour Foundation*

Meekness is not a quality we think to strive for. It's not flashy, it's hardly sexy. But we can't say we want to be like Jesus and overlook the very characteristic he used to describe himself. Meek Not Weak digs deep to uncover the hidden gem of meekness, what it looks like, why it matters, and how it can radiate and reshape our lives.

—Rachel Allord, author of *Mother of My Son* and *The Ground Beneath Us*

Reader beware, this book you now hold in your hands just might change your life. From the moment I picked up Abigail's book Meek Not Weak, God started using it to point out areas of my life where I wasn't exhibiting meekness. It was a virtue I had forgotten, and maybe honestly, felt was for another time. But Abigail's gentle, clear, and thoroughly biblical explanations and examples of meekness brought it into new daily focus for me. This is a book I will use, recommend, and return to often. It's a must-read for all who want to grow to be more like the One who is meek and lowly of heart.

—Cara Ray, author of *Paths of the Righteous*

You know when you read something that really resonates and convicts and your highlighter is almost dry from all of the passages you have underlined? That's how I feel about this study.

—Kendra Rose

Meek Not Weak turned all my assumptions about the weakness of meekness on their head, teaching Scripturally and clearly what a fought-for strength meekness is. Compelling, honest, and beautifully written, Meek Not Weak will make you look at everything—your own life, culture, what the Bible says about the True Meek One—and see either the lack or evidence of meekness there.

—Hannah MacAskill

I learned so much through this study of a rarely discussed topic. I knew that Jesus was both meek and mighty. But Abigail showed me, through Scripture and Christ's example, what it looks like for me to be meek in daily life, and how that reflects Christ to others. Meekness is the perfect blend of confidence and trust, of humility and strength, but it doesn't come naturally to us. It can only come from knowing Christ.

—Cheryl Balcom, writer and blogger

Abigail took the nebulous concept of meekness and opened up for me what it is, and what it isn't. Now I find myself working meekness into conversations knowing the change of hearts and lives that a true, biblical understanding of meekness brings.

—Terre Sortyka, participant in the pilot Meek Not Weak group study

"The meek are the strong in the Lord who have been broken by God to his yoke; gentled to his use." I'm still pondering these words from Meek Not Weak. This book opened my eyes to meekness. It is a must-read for followers of Jesus. Beautifully and powerfully, Abigail unpacks what it means to model Christ Jesus in meekness. Be prepared to be tamed by God. You may even come away grateful for the times God said no.

—Precious Mast, author of *I Choose: A 31-Day Devotional*

This book may change your life. Abigail sifts the chaff of the world's confused definitions of strength from God's unchanging truth to bring the reader to a place of unmovable rest in His love and purpose.

—Myrt Marker

Meek Not Weak is one of the most practical Bible studies I have done. In addition to examples from the "Meek Masters" of the Bible, as well as Abigail's own life, one soon recognizes that meekness applies to literally every area of our lives! Working through this study with a group of women was invaluable. Not only did we help one another to identify ways to apply meekness, but we also supported one another with the acknowledgment that putting on meekness is no easy task, but can be done with God's strength and the working of the Holy Spirit.

—Sandra Venden, participant in the pilot Meek Not Weak group study

Taking part in this study has helped me be gracious at times when it does not come naturally. I'm learning to talk back to my feelings as I hold meekness close to my heart.

—Christin Milbradt, participant in the pilot Meek Not Weak group study

In Meek Not Weak, Abigail gives us a way to redeem the pain in our lives and turn it to gold. As I read about the great ones, the beloved ones—Moses, Joseph, Mary, Job and God's intimate involvement in their lives, I came to understand that I too am one of the beloved ones. God is as intimately involved in my life as He was in theirs. What a wonderful truth! What could be better?

—Cynthia Mooney

New joy from the Lord bubbled in me as I followed Abigail through Meek Not Weak. Delight came again and again as I was offered a transformed vision of life's roadblocks. The reflection questions gently challenged me to find and welcome a deeper application of God's workings in my life. Abigail's openness and vulnerability create a safe haven for the reader.

—Rebecca Kordatzky, author of *Loving Him More Through the Darkest Valleys*

Many authors have written about the fruit of the Spirit and its sweetness. Abigail has opened up this fruit and revealed the fruit's center...MEEKNESS. Overlooked and underappreciated, meekness is that hard, strong core of the fruit from which other fruitful characteristics emanate and ripen. Meek Not Weak has been a providential tool to strengthen my spiritual "core." I highly recommend this study for anyone serious about their spiritual growth.

—Robert Leafblad, M.Ed., Christian Life Coach

ABIGAIL WALLACE

MEEK NOT WEAK

A 12-Week Guide to the
Gentle Strength of Meekness

Cover & interior design by Typewriter Creative Co.

Scripture quotations are from The ESV® Bible (The Holy Bible, English Standard Version®), copyright © 2001 by Crossway, a publishing ministry of Good News Publishers. Used by permission. All rights reserved.

ISBN 979-8-9870444-0-7 (Paperback)
ISBN 979-8-9870444-1-4 (eBook)

This book is dedicated to

*Jesus Christ, the mighty King of meekness and to
all the meek saints who dwell in the land.*

*The world's ideal is, on the whole, very different from His.
It inclines to the more conspicuous and so-called heroic virtues; it
prefers a great, flaring, yellow sunflower to the violet hiding among
the grass, and making its presence known only by fragrance. 'Blessed
are the strong, who can hold their own,' says the world.*

'Blessed are the meek,' says Christ.

—Alexander MacLaren

TABLE OF CONTENTS

WARNING

This book is intended to stretch you. It was written to help you grow through whatever God sends you. We'll touch on big theological topics like providence and suffering that won't be finally settled until we see Jesus face to face. Some of its descriptions of meekness will leave you scratching your head and checking your heart. There will be raised eyebrows. As I've worked my way through the book, writing it, reading it, re-writing it, rereading it, I can assure you that it makes me squirm, but more in a ticklish than a painful way. Because after the initial discomfort that comes from seeing how far I fall short in reflecting Christ's meekness, I hear this same Lord Jesus gently calling me back. *Come to me, I am meek and humble. Take my yoke, learn from me.*

Read *Meek Not Weak* on your own or with a group. Readers have done it both ways and both report that taking time to reflect and answer the chapter-end questions has been invaluable in shaping a life-transforming, trial-redeeming meek mindset.

If you have any questions or comments regarding the content in this book, I'd love to hear from you. You can contact me at joyfullypressingon@gmail.com, Instagram @AbigailWallace.4 or Facebook at Abigail Wallace.

Additional Resources For Meek Not Weak

- Free printable "My Meekness Profile" short form
- Free downloadable Psalm 37:1-11 meekness Bible study guide
- Free #meekgeek printable 8x11 Quest for Meekness quotes/Bible verses

Meek Not Weak is biography of meekness—the too-long neglected Spirit fruit that converts resistance and resentment over circumstances we cannot control into supernatural peace and joy. Used to his hand, and tamed by his grace, the meek face trials with the gentle, freeing strength.

Meek Not Weak is for Christ followers who are intentional about spiritual growth. They strive to grow stronger in faith as they take God at his Word. They grapple to find where divine sovereignty and human responsibility intersect and long to see God's hand and enjoy his peace in all things. They talk back to themselves and like to say, "Not somehow, but victoriously."

Warning: don't read this book if you don't like a challenge. It is not for the faint of heart. *Meek Not Weak* is not for those content with their current spiritual state, for those whose approach to spiritual growth is "let go and let God." Rather, it is for those who welcome the Spirit's conviction, and who, more than anything on earth, want to be conformed to the image of Jesus.

Oh good. You're still reading. I offer you my heartfelt thanks for opening this book. I pray that it will be one of God's gracious means to tame you.

Yes. I meant that. To *tame* you.

Let me explain. *Meek* comes from an ancient word that means "tamed wild animal." Over time, meekness has been badly misunderstood. Most people today think it means weak—easy to push around. But it actually means the opposite.

Who even are the meek? We know how a tame animal acts. But what about a tame person? Would you be able to pick one out? Because there are meek among us.

They're the ones who give up the last word, who don't insist on their way. When they hear the doctor say, *"I'm sorry,"* they've trained themselves to think, *"It must be for my good."* Whether waiting for a long train to pass or *that* coupon lady at the store, they can wait because they know the Time Redeemer. They hold their plans loosely and bend like a willow tree, which also makes them excellent friends. They sift your words, *chaff and grain together*—they keep what is worth keeping and with a breath of kindness, let the rest blow away. They've got soft hearts and thick skin and are slow to take offense. They're the least defensive people on the planet. They don't fret when the bad guys prosper or take revenge. They trust that the Judge of the Earth will do right and they wait patiently for him to act. They forgive first, cover in love and overcome evil with good. They bake cookies for their enemies. They are pillows who absorb blows and know how to quiet their souls. They really rejoice with those who rejoice, *without* self-pity and envy. *Deserve* and *entitled* are dirty words to them, because *everything* is a gift. But they courageously defend the weak, and are lambs when it comes to defending themselves but lions for the cause of Christ. Fear of being denied doesn't keep them from making bold requests, but when God says "No," they move on, *without* sulking or resentment. *God has his good reasons*, they say, *and it doesn't matter if I see them all.* They are patient and calm, humble and gentle, strong and self-controlled. They overcome.

That description took 278 words. But there is one word that describes these people: *Meek*.

The meek are those tamed by the God's Spirit; they yield to his hand. With Jesus Christ, God's Son, they *delight* to do the Father's will (Hebrews 10:7, John 8:29).

"Still, what is the big deal about meekness?" Here is why quiet, unassuming meekness matters. Our Lord Jesus didn't self identify with too many words. But he did say, "I am meek and lowly in heart" (Matthew 11:29, King James Bible). He beckons, *Come to me, learn from me, share my yoke* (Matthew 11:28). As we learn from him, our souls find rest.

But this rest comes with a yoke. A yoke is a heavy wooden bar that fits over the neck of an ox so that it can pull a cart or a plow. In a shared yoke, one ox might be much stronger than the other. It was more schooled in the commands of the master and so it would guide the other according to the master's commands. The weaker ox learned to obey the master's voice by sharing the yoke. Meekness is easily yielding to the Father's will and gladly sharing Christ's yoke. It is the taming grace that helps us rest in, and not resist, God's wise, loving hand.

Whether your soul is provoked by another season of waiting or a toddler's tirade, by unfair criticism or by chronic pain, "breaking meek" is the way to triumph. Not despite, but through circumstances you did not choose. I pray that *Meek Not Weak* is a path to the fresh joy and abundant peace that God promises to all the happy, blessed meek.

As you begin the journey into this neglected and overlooked Spirit-fruit, my heart's desire is that the words of this old Puritan prayer[1] would increasingly become the cry of our hearts.

> *Help me to see how good thy will is in all,*
> *And even when it crosses mine*
> *Teach me to be pleased with it.*
> *Grant me to feel thee in fire, and food and every providence,*
> *And to see that thy many gifts and creatures*
> *Are but thy hands and fingers taking hold of me.*

————————

With you, for our progress and joy in the faith,

Abigail

MY MEEKNESS PROFILE

How meek are you? Take the "My Meekness Profile" to find out. For items 1-20, circle every item that is true for you "more often than not." Ask a trusted friend for feedback if you're not sure. Score 1 point for each "yes" answer.

This profile is intended to help you recognize meekness, not to compare yourself with others. To help you celebrate growth, compare your score now with your score after 12 weeks.

1. I receive criticism and look for the "kernel of truth" even if my critic seems off-base.

2. I ask friends or family for help or favors even when I'm not sure they'll say yes.

3. I let insensitive words from others roll off me "like water off a duck's back."

4. I try to respond right away when the Word of God convicts me.

5. I get more angry when God is dishonored rather than when I am disrespected.

6. I more often think, Why not me? than, Why me? when I'm inconvenienced.

7. I make a habit of confessing my sins in specifics to God or others.

8. I give the benefit of the doubt and assume the best when someone lets me down.

9. I give others the last word in debates and discussions.

10. I give up my rights and accept less than I paid for without a fuss.

11. I go with the flow when plans change unexpectedly.

12. I seek more to "win the person" than to "win the argument."

13. I generally weigh my words and pause before I speak my mind.

14. I tend to have a longer fuse than most of those around me.

15. I tend to think, when a train or a head cold slows me down, There must be a good reason.

16. I seek to make peace first in a conflict or misunderstanding.

17. I remember the last time I said, I was wrong. Please forgive me.

18. I trust God's love even when painful things are happening to me.

19. I generally find it as easy to rejoice with others as to weep with them.

20. I am approachable.

FOR QUESTIONS 21-30, ask yourself, *"Would my spouse or close friends, if they were being totally honest, say that more than the "average person, I ______."* Circle every "no" answer, and give yourself one point for each "no."

21. I need to be in control.

22. I have a hard time moving on and accepting forgiveness.

23. I am harsh when I correct others.

24. I am assertive for my rights.

25. I am "high-maintenance."

26. I am outspoken.

27. I am hypersensitive to criticism.

28. I am hurt when those I serve don't thank me.

29. I am defensive.

30. I am impatient.

SCORING

A: "Yes" answers from 1-20: _______

B: "NO" answers from 21-30:_______

TOTAL A + B = _______

- A score of 26-30 means you've got the meekness of Moses.
- 16-25 means your meekness quotient is above average.
- 10-15 means average meekness.
- Under 10? *MEEK NOT WEAK* is a good-fit book for you!

Regardless of your score, *MEEK NOT WEAK* will bolster you and help increase your score.

MEEK MATTERS

1 - Meekness & Me

I chafed against God's control over my closed womb. I resisted His hand. The conflict in my church and in my marriage—that *He* had allowed—nearly consumed me. I did *not* gladly accept God's ways with me. I tried to twist my story arc back to fit *my* script. I was mad. I resented those who had hurt my feelings and blocked my way. If meekness is yielding to God's hand, then I was not meek.

WHY MEEKNESS

Fast forward twelve years. God did not reopen my womb. Marital conflict continued. We were not reconciled to our church. Life sped on. We loved and served in another church. My friends and family members kept having more babies. I was busy with my part-time job and Christian ministry and being a mom. I was an exile huffing through the wilderness, far from meek.

Then one wintry morning, running in the basement on the treadmill, I caught a podcast on—of all things—meekness. The host quoted from a 300-year-old book by Matthew Henry[3] that she'd been reading,

> *It is for lack of meekness that we are so impatient of contradiction in our opinions, in our desires, in our designs.*

That caught my attention. She quoted again:

> *Men's reproaches are God's rebukes, and whoever he be that affronts me, I must see and say that therein my Father corrects me.*

My ears were burning now. People had mistreated me, but I'd never thought of that as a rebuke or some form of correction from God.

She continued,

> *When the events of providence are grievous and afflictive, meekness not only quiets us under them but reconciles us to them, and enables us not only to bear but to receive evil as well as good at the hand of the Lord. It is to kiss the rod.*

I slowed to a walk so I could take this in. Then the zinger, the clincher, the jaw-dropper came.

> *Such is the law of meekness that whatsoever pleases God must not displease us. Let Him do what He will, for He will do what is best, and therefore, if God should refer the matter to me, says the meek and quiet soul, being well assured that He knows what is good for me better than I do for myself, I would refer it to Him again.*

I was breathless, and not because I had picked up my pace. No. Because, like a lightning bolt, it hit me, I needed meekness.

Patience, yes, endurance, yes, forgiveness, yes. I knew I needed those and I'd been working on and praying for those. But meekness? This was new.

So I ordered that 300-year-old book, "The Quest for Meekness and Quietness of Spirit." I pored over it—nearly all of its 144 pages are dog-eared and well-marked—and was deeply moved by Henry's message:

> *We must learn to walk with meekness, for this is "in the sight of God of great price." Therefore this mark of honor is, in a special measure, put upon the grace of meekness, because it is commonly despised and looked upon with contempt by the children of this world.... Meekness... is a very excellent grace which every one of us should put on.*

I was starved for peace. Because meekness matters to God, suddenly meekness mattered to me. Meekness came alive for me that morning on the treadmill.

Do you remember the story of the four Israeli lepers who lived in the prophet Elisha's day? These unfortunate men were starving and outcast as their city was under siege. Desperate, they went to the enemy camp prepared if not to find mercy, then to face death. But when they reached the edge of the camp, they found it abandoned. You can read along in 2 Kings 7:8-9a (New International Version),

> *The men who had leprosy reached the edge of the camp, entered one of the tents and ate and drank. Then they took silver, gold and clothes, and went off and hid them. They returned and entered another tent and took some things from it and hid them also. Then they said to each other, "What we're doing is not right. This is a day of good news and we are keeping it to ourselves.*

Well, that was meekness and me in those first delicious days of epiphany. It almost felt like plundering. For months I stole in and feasted on what seemed like abandoned treasure. I just couldn't keep it to myself. After taking silver and gold from that "first tent"—a 300-year-old book about meekness by Matthew Henry—I went back searching for more. I devoured every sermon and podcast, every article and blog post on meekness that I could find. I took notes and more notes as I unearthed one meek gem after another. Each nugget, a redemptive truth that assured me that my hardships weren't accidental, meaningless or wasted. Infertility and estrangement persisted, but meekness was a balm that allowed me to *grow*, not merely *go*, through them.

Meek Not Weak was born of the conviction that I couldn't keep this good thing—this neglected, but "first-place grace"—to myself. So I had to introduce meekness to my friends, one beggar showing others where to find bread. In the context of a weekly ladies' Bible study, I introduced meekness to my girlfriends. In those months we studied and questioned and found ourselves being transformed. I watched contentment and peace gradually displace resentment and self-pity as the women gained a biblical vision of meekness. Our assertive, willful spirits were coming under control of God's hand. We were becoming more meek.

Why did I write this book? Because meekness has transformed the way I perceive trials. I'm *learning* to welcome them as God-sent tools to conform me into the image of Jesus. I *know* I'm not alone in my ache to redeem and not waste every trouble I face. Meekness allows us to do this—not only to endure but to score off of our afflictions. In other words, when we receive the hard people and difficult circumstances in our lives with meekness, we are more Christlike than we would have been without facing them. Which is exactly why we're here, right? To be conformed to the image of Jesus *is* God's good purpose for us (Romans 8:28-29).

We become what we behold. Which means that if we want to *be* more meek, we've got to see the meek. We are changed from glory to glory *by* beholding the glory of the Lord (2 Corinthians 3:18).

I wrote *Meek Not Weak* for two reasons:

1. **Information:** To cast the clear, compelling vision of biblical meekness; and

2. **Transformation:** So that in seeing this strong grace, you'll be conformed to the image of Jesus. When Christ is exalted, God gets the glory.

I've been writing this book for ten years. Looking back, though, it seems to have been *writing me.*

WHY ME?

"What, other than your treadmill journey and your small group experience, qualifies *you* to write a book-length work about meekness, Ms. Abigail?"

I'm so glad you asked. Abuse victims write books for victims of abuse. Former addicts address struggling addicts. Recovering alcoholics write for alcoholics desperate for help. Trim figures who've lost half their body weight compel trim wannabes. Former over-spenders forced into bankruptcy are mad about budgets. Healed hoarders could wax endlessly about custom closets.

That's meekness and me.

I'm not naturally meek. No one is. But left to myself, I'm the anti-type for meek. I tested "way-A" on the high school personality test. Coach Barry assured us that Type A's make great athletes because of temperaments "characterized by excessive ambition, competitiveness, impatience, and need for control." Bold A's present a confident, assertive, and decisive image to others. No wonder driven triple-A's dominate.

For years I blamed birth order for my take-charge personality. I am, after all, a first-born and the first grandchild on both sides. Add to that the status that comes from being a pastor's kid and a sprinkling of academic and athletic success and you have a recipe for a pretty self-confident kid who would grow into an assertive young woman. Left untamed, I became a headstrong and stubborn, resistant and resentful woman toward anyone or any circumstance that blocked my way.

While this book is deeply personal, it is not a memoir. Nor is it self-help. Rather, it's my humble attempt to paint a portrait of biblical meekness that makes others want to be more meek. You could say *Meek Not Weak* is a biography of biblical meekness. In it, you'll see snapshots of the meekness that the Holy Spirit of Jesus has used to tame and transform this impatient, take-matters-into-my-own-hands, firstborn, Type-A Christian into a meek child of the God, accustomed to the *Father's guiding hand*, ever conforming to the image of Jesus.

GOD'S VISION FOR MEEKNESS

We must behold his glory to be transformed by it. God's glory includes the paradoxical lion-lamb, strength under control, mighty meek glory. God made us with eyes for beauty, eyes to savor His glory. Meekness is a glory peculiar to Christian eyes; eyes unveiled by the Holy Spirit to see its splendor. To the ordinary eye, meekness is as despised and rejected as the One who meekly *bore our griefs and carried our sorrows*. Without kingdom eyes, meekness is as lovely as mud. Lovely as *the scarred and rejected One*.

Meek Not Weak is one spiritual-strength-seeker confessing that she chased strength up the wrong tree. But she climbed down and now lives giddy to declare: "I've been up that control tree. Strength is not there. You will never believe where I found real power!" Meeting meekness has transformed my vision. I now see meekness, or the absence of it, in almost every interaction in which I take part. I hear it or the lack of it in hard times and while facing difficult people. I see God's vision for meekness in the life of Christ-followers.

Meekness applies both to our relationship with God and others. It touches everything. It transforms trials into triumphs. It's how we cheerfully choose what we did not choose and learn to *count it all joy*. Meekness is the strong, unsung grace that tames our impatient, strong-willed, sinful nature.

Bible teacher Nancy DeMoss-Wolgemuth[4] explains how meekness affects:

- the way we respond to people
- the way we respond to pressures
- the way we respond to problems
- the way we respond to the providence of God, His choices in our lives
- the way we respond to poverty or to prosperity

To some degree, our response to every challenge in life is determined by our meekness. When we are spiritually made over by meekness, we can say to the Lord in the face of every pressure and problem, every trial and trouble:

If it pleases you, it pleases me. I wouldn't have picked this. I wouldn't have written my story this way, and I don't have to understand. I accept the circumstances you have brought into my life. All your ways are good.

I pray that a compelling, biblical portrait of meekness will unfold in the following weeks and that by the grace of God and to the praise of His beloved meek Son, you will grow more meek. In what feels like an increasingly hostile *and* fragile world, meekness matters now more than ever.

MEEKNESS HALL OF FAITH

If you choose to seek meekness you'll find some elite company. Yet meekness is for *every single* saint. Meekness is a trait that in some measure marks every child of God, for, "Blessed are the meek," Christ said, and "The fruit of the spirit is... meekness." When Christ dwells in us, we too will be among the blessed, happy, well-off meek. We join those to whom Jesus says, as it were, "Congratulations! You're becoming a lot like me."

<u>**We will learn to say...**</u>

- **With the Psalmist** (Psalm 119:71, 75), *"It was good for me that I was afflicted, that I might keep your Word...In righteousness you afflicted me."*

- **With Job**, after his health and wealth were destroyed and his children had died (Job 1:21), *"The Lord gives and the Lord takes away, blessed be the name of the Lord."* And later (Job 23:10), *"He knows the way I take; when he has tried me, I shall come forth as gold."*

- **With Moses** when Miriam grumbled against him and the Lord made her leprous (Numbers 12:13), *"O God, please heal her—please."*

- **With Joseph** to his brothers who sold him into slavery (Genesis 15:20), *"You intended it for evil but God intended it for good, that he might save many people."*

- **With David**, as he fled Jerusalem and Absalom (2 Samuel 15:26), *"Let [the LORD] do to me as seems good to him,"* and later when God punished him (2 Samuel 24:14), *"Let me fall into the hands of God."*

- **With Mary**, when she and God alone knew she was a virgin (Luke 1:38), *"May it be to me according to your word, O Lord."*

- **With Stephen** in the midst of a murderous pelt of stones, who prayed to the Lord who had prayed the same way (Acts 6:15), *"Do not hold this against them."*

- **With Paul**, who from his jail cell chose to rejoice rather than to resent those responsible for his unjust imprisonment and wrote (Philippians 2:12,18), *"I want you to know, brothers, that what has happened to me has really served to advance the gospel...The important thing is that in every way, whether from false motives or true, Christ is preached. And because of this I rejoice."*

- **And with our Lord Jesus Christ**, who moments before he was arrested, knelt down and prayed (Luke 22:42), *"Father, if you are willing, take this cup from me; yet not my will, but yours be done."*

> We don't say, "I don't deserve this," and we shouldn't say, "I do deserve this." We should say, "I need this." That is the spirit of meekness.
>
> —Jerry Bridges[2]

Friends, we were created for God's glory (Isaiah 43:7, Matthew 5:16, Ephesians 1:6-7). When we clothe ourselves with the cloak of meekness we resemble not only this company of meek, faithful saints, but Jesus Christ, the Son of God. Like no other grace, meekness transforms us to the Son's image. And *that* brings glory to God the Father.

When you choose meekness you stand in the company of all these meek heroes of faith.

This is meekness—the Spirit fruit and taming grace for our resistant, resentful, wild rebel souls.

This is power under Christ's control.

Meet meekness.

FOR FURTHER REFLECTION

1. Before this study, would you have described yourself as "meek"? Why or why not?

2. *Such is the law of meekness that whatsoever pleases God must not displease us. Let Him do what He will, for He will do what is best, and therefore, if God should refer the matter to me, says the meek and quiet soul, being well assured that He knows what is good for me better than I do for myself, I would refer it to Him again.* This was quoted in that life-changing podcast. How does this statement strike you? Does it seem possible to see life this way? What would it take to have this kind of perspective on the hard people and difficult circumstances in life?

3. Read 1 Peter 3:4. This verse says "a meek (or gentle), and quiet spirit, is of great worth in God's sight." Why do you think God places such a high value on meekness?

4. *Meekness is a glory peculiar to Christian eyes.* Do you agree with that statement? Why would it be the case that Christian eyes would see meekness as such a beautiful virtue?

5. *Meekness allows us to score off our afflictions.* It allows us not only to endure them, but to grow stronger through them. How could this possibly be? How does responding to difficult events with meekness actually make us stronger?

6. Review the list of meek Bible characters described in the last page. If time allows, look up the references and read the context for each quote. Describe how each character showed meekness. Can you think of other meek characters in the Bible? Or other Bible verses that express a sense of strength yielded to God's will and under his control?

7. *To some degree, our response to every challenge in life is determined by our meekness.* What challenging situation are you facing that you want to respond to with meekness?

PRAYER OF RESPONSE

Dear Lord, thank you that you have called me to seek you and to know you better. Help me to see myself as I truly am, weak and helpless without you and bold as a lion in your righteousness. Help me to see the quiet glory of meekness and become more meek, because a meek and quiet spirit is precious in your sight.

Amen.

2 - Meekness Defined

"You know that you do have a strong personality, Abigail."

I winced. Not that my sister-in-law was wrong. I'm no pushover. And not that having a strong will is bad. I tell my friends how kids with strong wills are a good thing because they're not so swayed by peer pressure and can stand against wrong. But hearing it *said* still stung. Because it's one thing to admit it myself but quite another thing to have someone else call me out.

I won't pretend. That wasn't the first I'd heard the sentiment. There was that roommate at a college retreat who called me *incorrigible*. I had to look it up:

1. *incapable of being corrected, amended, or reformed*

2. *not manageable : unruly*

I had to admit, it fit. She flung the word at me because I wouldn't bend. I wouldn't wait. I couldn't be late, so off I charged—without her.

But expression of this strong trait of mine goes back further than that. As I grew up, my mom's most oft-repeated correction was, "Don't take matters into your own hands, Ab." That was especially hard when mom was at work and my siblings were slack in their work. Bossing drove my younger brother and sisters crazy. Repressing my boss mode made my assertive side ache.

More recently, like, say…today, I've been called a tornado. "Clean off the table, put away your screens. Get in gear, you guys," I barked upon arrival after a morning away. And last weekend, playing board games with my girlfriends, I broke a sweat trying to keep my pusher, driver competitive tendencies in check. Even then, one friend firmly and gently put me in my place: "Last hand. Sorry Ab. Jen has to get to bed." So we never did settle that best of three.

It's all true. God has given me a strong personality. In all my life, no one ever called me weak.

At least not to my face.

SUPER-CONQUERING STRENGTH

But that bulldozer, my-way-or-the-highway strong, isn't what God calls strong. Real biblical strength is found in union with Christ. It is seen more through the Spirit-produced self-control, than mustered up control over the people and situations around us. Our emotions and actions are not captive to our circumstances. We ride through our trials assured that in *all these things* we are "super-conquerors through Christ" (Romans 8:37).

That's Greek-speak for "more than conquerors." It means that through Christ we are actually triumphing not *despite*, but *because* of our trials. In other words, what would destroy and weaken the faith of some, bolsters and strengthens our faith. These things can even bring joy. Because, as James explains (James 1:2-4), they are purposeful. They come so that we will be mature and complete—and, get this—lack nothing.

Does that mean the meek feel no pain? Nope. Trials still try us. Afflictions still afflict. But the meek learn to rest knowing that God is always *for* his children (see Psalm 56:9, Romans 8:31).

The heavenly Father gives his children good things (Matthew 7:11).

The meek know that God's goodness and mercy follow them all the days of their lives. They rest in the storms of life; on the soft pillow of God's providence. In short, *they are used to God's hand.* They believe God has better plans for his children than they can see now. They trust he is always and in everything he is working for his glory and their good. Leaning into this makes them responsive to his hand.

If you take no other definition away from these 12 weeks, I hope you will take these two truths:

1. **Meekness is being accustomed to, or used to, God's hand.**

2. **The more we abide in Christ (see John 15:1-9), the more used to His guiding hand we will be.**

In fact, in the Latin translation of the Bible, called the Vulgate, the word we now read in English as *meekness* was translated *mansuetus*. It was a compound word that joined "manus" (hand) + "suetus" (accustomed; used to). Despite my affinity for the term, I'm not expecting *mansuetus* to make a comeback. It's archaic and hard to pronounce.

But meekness? If I have any say in the matter, it just might. But, pardon the language whiplash, it will involve a peek at Greek.

BIBLICAL USES OF MEEKNESS AND MEEK

Meekness is massively misunderstood in the world. Even within the church, few believers grasp the true meaning of meekness. Bible scholar William Barclay[3] shines a light on a possible reason why. Barclay suggests that *praütēs*, the Greek word often translated as *meek*, is one of "the most untranslatable of words in the New Testament."

The translation of *praütēs* might appear as *meekness, gentleness,* or *humility,* depending on which Bible version we read. Gentleness and humility, first cousins to meekness, are easier to define because they have clear opposites. The opposite of gentleness is harshness—a single word and easy to define. The opposite of humility is pride. Again, a single word antonym. But the opposite of meekness? No one-word opposite exists for meekness. A.W. Pink[4] used a full-length sentence to illuminate the flip side of meekness.

Meekness, he says, is *the opposite of self-will toward God, and of ill-will toward men.*

Consider the following verses featuring the Greek noun, *prautes,* pronounced prah-oo'-tace, which is translated as "meekness" or "gentleness."

1. *Put on then, as God's chosen ones, holy and beloved, compassionate hearts, kindness, humility, meekness, and patience* (Colossians 3:12).

2. *But the fruit of the Spirit is love, joy, peace, patience, kindness, goodness, faithfulness, meekness, self-control; against such things there is no law* (Galatians 5:22-23, American Standard Version).

3. *Therefore put away all filthiness and rampant wickedness and receive with meekness the implanted word, which is able to save your souls* (James 1:21).

4. *And the Lord's servant must not be quarrelsome but kind to everyone, able to teach, patiently enduring evil, correcting his opponents with meekness* (2 Timothy 2:24-25).

> No triumphant chariot is so easy, so safe, so truly glorious, as that in which the meek and quiet soul rides over all the provocations of an injurious world with a gracious unconcernedness.
>
> —Matthew Henry[2]

5. *I, Paul, myself entreat you, by the meekness and gentleness of Christ—I who am humble when face to face with you, but bold toward you when I am away!* (2 Corinthians 10:1)

6. *But in your hearts honor Christ the Lord as holy, always being prepared to make a defense to anyone who asks you for a reason for the hope that is in you; yet do it with meekness and respect* (1 Peter 3:15).

Praus, pronounced prah-ooce, is Greek for the adjective "meek." Sometimes *praus* is translated as "humble."

1. *Blessed are the meek, for they shall inherit the earth* (Matthew 5:5).

2. *Take my yoke upon you, and learn from me, for I am meek and lowly in heart, and you will find rest for your souls* (Matthew 11:29).

3. *Say to the daughter of Zion, 'Behold, your king is coming to you, meek, and mounted on a donkey, on a colt, the foal of a beast of burden* (Matthew 21:5).

4. *But let your adorning be the hidden person of the heart with the imperishable beauty of a meek and quiet spirit, which in God's sight is very precious* (1 Peter 3:4).

The concept of *prautēs* is what this book aims to reclaim. We call it meekness here to distinguish it from other Greek words that have similar, but not identical, meanings.

To be sure, the meek one will also be humble and gentle. After all, the fruit of the Spirit is one fruit. Galatians 5:22 is clear that it is "fruit" not "fruits" of the Spirit. Who has ever heard of a loving, peaceful, patient person who is not—at least to some degree—also kind, good, and self-controlled? While the English might use one of the overlapping terms, know that if *prautēs* is the Greek word behind it, the concept being described is meekness.

DIFFERENCES BETWEEN MEEKNESS, HUMILITY, & GENTLENESS

So what is the difference between *humility, gentleness,* and *meekness?* What a great question, especially since we've seen that the same Greek and—though we won't look at here—Hebrew words are sometimes translated into these same English words. While they are all Spirit-fruit "cousins"—think strawberries, blueberries, raspberries—there are distinctions among them.

Let's begin with this perspective. We could say that:

- *humility* is our view of ourselves before God — as creatures dependent on and under our Creator;
- *gentleness* is tender kindness toward people; and
- *meekness* is our trusting response of submission to God when we face difficult people or hard circumstances.

Think of the distinction this way. A star athlete can be humble atop the gold medal podium without being meek. A mother can be gentle cradling her baby without being meek. We can be humble and gentle when we are not being provoked, under strain or in the face of conflict. But to be meek is to be humble and gentle in the face of adversity.

THE GREEK BEHIND MEEK

Now let's head back to language class for a minute. In classical Greek, the origins of the word mean:

- *to tame or gentle a horse for harness;*
- *to break it for bridle.*

Horses are powerful animals but their power is useless unless it can be harnessed and bridled. The meek are the strong in the Lord who have been broken to Christ's yoke. The meek will he guide in justice; and the meek will he teach his way (Psalm 25:9, American Standard Version). They are gentled to God's use. Meekness is the opposite of unbridled emotion; but also the opposite of weak and mousy. The meek don't chafe, stiffen their necks or resist when God is dealing with them. Their virtue is born not of a weak nature, but of a strong character. They are gentle and calm, even while possessed of great strength.

> Meekness is strength under control. Biblical meekness is strength under the Holy Spirit's control.

Xenophon, an ancient Greek historian,[5] shed light on this aspect of meekness when he described a gift—a white stallion—from a young soldier to his fiancée during the Peloponnesian War (500-400 BC). The horse, he writes, is:

> *...the most magnificent animal I have ever seen. He responds obediently to the slightest command. He allows his master to direct him to his full potential...He is a meek horse.*

That soldier wasn't saying that the horse was timid or weak. Rather, this was an animal with great spirit; a spirit yielded to the rider. When a strong creature is tamed, and submits its strength to the master, this is meek.

One Bible dictionary[6] defines meekness as:

> *...an inwrought grace of the soul...in which we accept God's dealings with us as good, and therefore without disputing or resisting; we deal meekly with men, even with the insults and injuries which they may inflict, believing they are permitted and employed by Him for our chastening and purifying.*

The concept is so rich that a nutshell can't capture it. Listen to these theologians describe the flavors inside the shell.

1. *Meekness consists in a peaceful freedom from fretful anger and is based on trusting God and rolling all our ways onto God and waiting patiently for God.* (John Piper)[7]

2. *Meekness is an enlightened awareness of the sovereignty of God.* (Jerry Bridges)[8]

3. *Meekness is the humble strength of the man who has learned to submit to his difficulty.* (Ligon Duncan)[9]

4. *Meekness lays hold on the sovereign will of God as our supreme good, and delights in absolutely and perfectly conforming itself thereto.* (Alexander MacLaren)[10]

5. *Meekness is choosing the way of patient faith instead of self-assertion.* (Derek Kidner)[11]

6. *Meekness is the easy and quiet submission of the soul to the whole will of God as He is pleased to make it known whether by His Word or by His providence.* (Matthew Henry)[12]

7. *Meekness is forged into a person by the way in which they bow themselves to the will of God as he reveals it in his Word and in the providences of life.* (Sinclair Ferguson)[13]

8. *Meekness is that temper of spirit in which we accept God's dealings with us as good, and therefore without disputing or resisting.* (Rod Mattoon)[14]

9. *Meekness is a spirit of patient submission and humility before all providences, produced by abdication of personal rights, manifesting itself in a spirit of gentleness.* (John Blanchard)[15]

10. *Meekness is a combination of patience, gentleness and complete submission to the will of God. It is learning to be self-controlled rather than needing to be in control. It is the firm resolve that it is always better to suffer than to sin.* (Kevin DeYoung)[16]

The English word "meekness," as we've seen already, comes from the Greek word prautes, which depicts the attitude or demeanor of a person who is forbearing, patient, and slow to respond in anger; one who remains in control of himself in the face of insults or injuries. Although provoking situations naturally produce angry outbursts or inner unrest, in a meek person they do not. They learn to submit their big dreams and high hopes, their little wishes and daily plans to a higher authority. They believe that God is good and that he does good (Psalm 119:68). They learn to align their hopes with the will of God. That is how the meek hold their peace and rest content in the storms of life.

In some ways, meekness is best defined by what it is not. Meekness is the opposite of self-assertion, of acting as if my will should trump God's and triumph over the will of my fellow man. Therefore, author Tim Challies[17] explains:

> *[I]t is the opposite of grumbling against God's providence as it's expressed through circumstances or even through the hands of men.*

The Apostle Paul's statement in Philippians 4:12-13 gives us a clear glimpse of this aspect of meekness:

> *I have learned in whatever situation I am to be content. I know how to be brought low, and I know how to abound. In any and every circumstance, I have learned the secret of facing plenty and*

hunger, abundance and need. I can do all things through him who strengthens me.

Given the context of Paul's often quoted, "I can do all things," we see that the strength offered is *not* the power to achieve our dreams or take first place. Rather, he is giving another description of meekness: contentment in the "brought low" and the "in need" times. A meek person may possess a powerful character and hold strong opinions, but as the Holy Spirit renews and transforms him, contentment is no longer determined by circumstances. He is then meek, not weak.

For the ancient Greeks meekness was a compliment for a horse, but in a person it was no virtue. They had no respect for the meek, for they associated it with a groveling servility—"Yes, ma'am. Whatever you say, sir." But the more we study biblical meekness, the more we will see how wrong they were. For the Christian, there may be no virtue with greater power to transform us into the likeness of Jesus. Perhaps this is why meekness is called "a first place grace."[18]

In the next chapter we'll see why meekness is essential for every disciple of Jesus Christ.

FOR FURTHER REFLECTION:

1. That bulldozer, my-way-or-the-highway strong, isn't what God calls strong. Real biblical strength is mastering oneself. Someone has said that *impatient people are weak people.* Where do self-control and patience fit into your concept of biblical strength? How does *patience* jibe with the world's definition of strength? What people or situations most challenge your patience? What or who helps you exercise more self-control in these situations?

2. Now consider that aspect of meekness as "strength under control," as in a spirited war horse that could be easily directed by its trainer's click of the tongue or soft command. How does this metaphor enhance your understanding of meekness as it relates to God?

3. Being slow to anger, as God is, touches near the core of meekness. Read and discuss the following passages as they relate to this aspect of meekness:

- Proverbs 16:32

- Proverbs 25:28

- Proverbs 19:11

- Psalm 103:8

- James 1:19

- Ephesians 4:26

4. Read through the 10 descriptions of meekness provided in this chapter. What words or themes are repeated in them? Which ones make the most sense to you?

5. Reread Philippians 4:10-13. Contentment is a peace and joy that comes from knowing and abiding in Christ (John 15:4). It is not dependent on people or circumstances. We could say meekness is the face of contentment when we are in need or in want. How did Paul show meekness in Philippians 1:12-23?

6. How would you describe the similarities and differences between the traits of *humility, gentleness,* and *meekness*? How would each be expressed toward people? Toward God?

7. The Latin word for meekness is *mansuetude*, a compound word made of "manus" (hand) + "suetus" (accustomed; used to). The more we abide in Christ (see John 15:1-9), the more used to his hand we become. Oswald Chambers wrote, "Jesus was at home with God wherever his body was placed. He never chose His own circumstances, but was meek towards His Father's [will for him]." What do you think it would look like for you to become more meek, more "used to" God's hand, in a situation you're facing today?

PRAYER OF RESPONSE

Dear Heavenly Father, thank you that you loved me so much that you called me and made me alive when I was a slave to myself, rebellious and wild. I thank you, too, that you loved me too much to leave me that way. Thank you for changing me, taming me and bringing my strength under your control. I want to be broken in such a way that I become used to your fatherly hand.

Amen.

3 - Meekness Matters

"It sounds like you see meekness everywhere," my husband declared recently after I shared my latest book progress. He was right—I do. When I bought my first car, suddenly I noticed all the cars that looked just like mine. When it gets personal, we notice.

Meekness is almost always on my mind, like a guide. When I wait to reply to a text, when I don't push my agenda, when I hear hard words and give up the last word—this is only because I see meekness. I reflect the meek and humble Jesus I've seen. "I have set the Lord always before me, because he is at my right hand, I will not be shaken" (Psalm 16:8a).

Discovering meekness has transformed my spiritual vision. Through the Holy Spirit's cultivating work, I now see meekness, or the absence of it, in nearly all my interactions. I hear it, or a lack of it, in hard times and with difficult people. Meekness applies to our relationships with God and with others. When I embrace the reality that every, and I do mean every, provoking circumstance and irritating person is an opportunity to grow more meek, meekness turns my trials to triumph. Through Christ and for his glory, meekness has materially transformed my life.

Those chances are abundant, right there for the taking, day in and day out. All in one recent day, meekness helped me hold my tongue when I wanted to set the record straight—*Be slow to speak*, I heard the whisper. Later, when the principal's third detention notice came—*It's for the best*, the Spirit said. At the end of the day, when a decade-old disappointment hit out of the blue, the words washed over me—*He does all things well*. But if we don't value meekness, we won't be able to seize the meek-making opportunities all around us.

> Meekness is more obvious than our love for God and our faith in Christ.
>
> —Matthew Henry[2]

Please don't misunderstand. Meekness does not magically make life easy or comfortable. But the meek know, in Paul Tripp's words[3], "that God is wise and he never gets the wrong address—he gives each of us exactly what we need." Only when we embrace this truth will we welcome the hard things in life we cannot control.

What about you? Still not sold? Here are five more reasons why meekness matters.

Reason #1: Because meekness makes you look more like Jesus.

Jesus chose every word he spoke with perfect care. He described himself with astounding clarity in Matthew 11:29 (King James Version),

> *I am meek and lowly of heart, learn from me.*

That is why meekness matters. Because of all the possible attributes he could have used to identify himself, Jesus chose meekness. Sinclair Ferguson[4] has said that this is "virtually the only personal quality about himself to which Jesus drew specific attention."

Jesus lived out meekness, "strength under control," perfectly. God's Son had access to the same power that created the world with a word. From his temptation in the wilderness to his temptation in the garden and every provocation in between, Jesus yielded his strength to the Father's control. When accused of being a drunkard and a glutton he said *wisdom is proved right by her actions*; when accused of breaking the Sabbath, he responded *read what the Scriptures say*; when transported to Jerusalem for Holy Week, he rode in *meek, on the foal of a donkey*; when mocked by Herod and led like a lamb to slaughter, *he was silent, and did not open his mouth*. That is meekness. Jesus entrusted himself to him who judges justly. He suffered and died on the cross, mistreated and misunderstood between two thieves. The cross is the emblem of meekness.

Kings, queens and people of influence throw their weight behind worthy causes like literacy, disaster relief or veterans' health hoping that others will stand behind these causes. In Psalm 45 we see Israel's mighty King standing for three causes.

> *In your majesty ride out victoriously for the cause of truth and meekness and righteousness; let your right hand achieve awesome deeds!*

Isn't this remarkable? Of all the possible causes, the psalmist chose to champion meekness (Psalm 45:4). Since Jesus the God-man born to be king, it is not surprising that he would affirm the blessings of meekness and self-identify as meek.

Our Lord was clear about the response he sought from his astounding self-description: learn from me. Jesus doesn't just want to be admired, he wants to be *imitated*. "Whoever claims to live in him must walk as Jesus did" (1 John 2:6). We are children of the Heavenly Father and brothers and sisters of Jesus (Hebrews 2:11; Romans 8:29; Mark 3:34). Our heavenly Father wants all His children to share a family resemblance, so he gave us the perfect example in our big brother, Jesus.

As the Holy Spirit works in us, we will increasingly be conformed to the image of Christ (Romans 8:29). We will learn from Jesus (Matthew 11:29). We will be more meek. The more meek we become, the more we look like Jesus, the King of meekness.

Reason #2: Because God promises abundant blessings for the meek.

God motivates his children to seek meekness by revealing blessings like these.

1. **Fresh Joy in the Lord:** In Isaiah 29:19 we read, "The meek shall obtain fresh joy in the Lord." The meek know that every circumstance can become a means of knowing God better and experiencing more of His grace. The meek know from experience that hard times and difficult people become "the chariots of God" to bring them closer to the One in whose presence is the fullness of joy (Psalm 16:11). Since this world provides new troubles each day, the meek have a continuous fountain of joy. "A meek and quiet Christian enjoys himself. He enjoys his friends. He enjoys his God,"

Matthew Henry[5] wrote. "And he puts it out of the reach of his enemies to disturb him in these enjoyments."

2. **Abundant Peace of God:** In Psalm 37:11 we read, "The meek will...delight themselves in abundant peace." The meek have hearts at rest because they are yoked together with the Prince of Peace. In Matthew 11:28-29 (King James Bible), He said, "Come to me, all who labor and are heavy laden, and I will give you rest. Take my yoke upon you, and learn from me, for I am meek and lowly in heart, and you will find rest for your souls." Matthew Henry[6] says it this way: "The work of meekness is to calm the spirit so that the inward peace may not be disturbed by any outward provocation." Yoked with Christ, the meek find peace: peace of mind, peace with others, peace with God. Oh yes, the meek enjoy great peace.

3. **Guidance from God:** In Psalm 25:9 we read, "The meek He will guide in judgment: the meek He will teach his way." Who among us doesn't desire more wisdom from above? Greater discernment? More divine guidance? A meek, humble spirit is a prerequisite for God's guidance. Teaching on this verse, Pastor John Piper[7] noted, "If you ask me, 'How can I know the will of God?' I will say, 'Admit all known sin and humble yourself under the mighty hand of God.'" This humility before God is central to meekness. The humble-meek have teachable spirits. We are unable to discern God's direction when our souls are puffed up; not capable of guidance when we are large and in charge. He leaves the proud to their own paths, but the Lord guides the meek.

One day, Jesus promised, the meek will inherit the whole earth (Matthew 5:5). Until then, fresh joy, abundant peace and divine guidance are great spiritual rewards promised to the meek. In chapter 12 we'll explore more tangible ways the meek inherit this present earth. Then *and* now: happy indeed. *Blessed are the meek.*

Reason #3: Because meekness makes you more useful to God.

Grandpa Al kept ponies. He kept the ones no one else would keep. There was a swayback who always garnered our sympathy but couldn't hold us on his back. And Rover, a 20-year old pony with flaring hooves, was too frail to carry anything. Then there was Jack the Kicker. Jack had the most potential to be useful— to be saddled or to get hitched to Grandpa's pony cart. He was young, strong, and able-bodied. But we never got to ride Jack because Jack kicked. Grandpa could never get him hitched. He would shake his head and warn, "Don't ever walk behind Jack or touch his backside."

While there was a certain allure to Grandpa's ponies, they were disappointing. You couldn't do anything with them. Especially Jack the Kicker. Jack did what Jack wanted to do because his brute strength would not be controlled.

Jack is why meekness matters. Meekness matters because wild ponies that kick and recoil at a touch do *not* win races, pull carts or give rides.

To be useful, one must be tamed, or "used to the hand." Remember the Latin word for meekness—*mansuetus*? It could refer to a once wild horse that has been tamed and is used to its trainer's hand. A horse that accepts a saddle or harness and is responsive to the trainer's commands—*Whoa, Easy, Back, Stand*—is a meek horse. Picture a Clydesdale drawing a carriage or a pony pulling a cart. It is useful for the task.

Pastor Colin Smith[8] says meekness "involves the taming of the temper, the calming of the passions, and the management of the impulses of our soul." It brings order out of the chaos in our souls. When we see it we want to be it. When we see how God beautifies the meek, we want to grow in meekness. And the more meek we become, the more useful we are to God. If it's *my way or the highway* and we chafe at God's hand, we will miss kingdom-building opportunities.

The more meek we grow, the more our strength is deployed in ways that reflect Christ's glory and bless the Father's heart. *Your kingdom come, your will be done, on earth and in me*, pray the meek, *as it is in heaven.*

Reason #4: Because meekness looks gorgeous on God's children.

Do you remember the book *Color Me Beautiful*?[9] If you're under 40 or male, you probably don't. It was wildly popular when I was a kid. When you wear your special, season-specific colors, the book promised, "you will indeed be the fairest of them all." I remember my mom poring over the color palettes, holding them next to her cheek. We agreed she was most beautiful "in the clear, true primary colors." I too seemed to receive compliments when I wore royal blue.

That's how meekness looks on the Christian. When we wear meekness, we look beautiful. We see that connection in Psalm 149:4: "For the LORD... will beautify the meek with salvation." In his commentary on that verse, C.H. Spurgeon[10] says, "When God himself beautifies a man, he becomes beautiful indeed and beautiful forever." There's just something about meekness. "Next to the beauty of holiness, which is the soul's agreement with God, is the beauty of meekness, which is the soul's agreement with itself," explains Matthew Henry.[11]

Jesus Christ himself calls us to learn his meekness. The Apostle Paul—himself an astounding example of a strong personality tamed by meekness—uses the language of clothing when he talks about meekness. In Colossians 3:12, he writes, "Put on, then, as God's chosen ones, holy and beloved, compassionate hearts, kindness, humility, meekness, and patience." Paul calls for meekness again in Ephesians 4:1-2 and Titus 3:2. Make no mistake, God wants his children dressed in meekness. He wants us gorgeously adorned.

The bold fisherman Peter was also transformed by the meekness of Jesus. It's not surprising then, that he took special note of the beauty of meekness. In 1 Peter 3:4 (American Standard Bible), he wrote that God's children should be dressed in "the incorruptible apparel of a meek and quiet spirit, which is in the sight of God of great price." Peter tells his readers that meekness brings an unfading beauty which is of great worth in God's sight.

Psalm 45 is a royal wedding Psalm. In it the bride is described as "all glorious...in colorful robes she is led to the king" (Psalm 45:13-14a). Meekness is one of the "colors" of the beautiful robes in which we, the Church, the bride of Christ, will be clothed.

Reason #5: Because the world is watching and it needs to see Jesus.

You might be the only Christian some of your friends or co-workers know. If they know you are a Christian, you represent Jesus to them. Their eyes are widest when your faith is tested.

When we worry and fret or become harsh and lash out without repentance, we show the watching world that God is not enough for *these* circumstances. He may have helped us through that last issue, but we need to manage this on our own. By our resistance we show that his grace is *not* sufficient for this difficult spouse or recurrent illness or frustrating boss. When life gets tough, does our response reveal trust in a God that is full of power and love (Psalm 62:11-12)?

For the meek, the answer is a resounding *yes*. They know that their circumstances are "the means of manifesting how wonderfully perfect...the Son of God is."[12] When we react to difficult people and tough circumstances with outraged entitlement, bitter resentment or the wounded pride of self-pity, we aren't reflecting the Lord we love and serve. But if we rest content in God's fatherly control, we witness without words. Whenever we react without turning around and reclaiming meekness, we give the world an impression of Jesus Christ. "It is in our trials," Matthew Henry[12] says, "that our meekness is more obvious than our love for God or our faith in Christ."

Puritan Richard Baxter[13] approaches it this way: "There are no virtues wherein your example will do more to lessen men's prejudices than humility, meekness and self-denial." He is spot on. A world that does not know Jesus notices the power in meekness when they see it. They may not have a name for it, but it is shockingly different from the ways of the world. There is nothing more powerful than our meekness to remove barriers to faith in general, and bias against believers in particular.

But what does our lack of meekness say? Does our response cause the watching world to second guess a Father we claim is faithful to all his promises and loving to all he has made (Psalm 145:13)? Or does it make them doubt a God who so loved the world (John 3:16) and is its only Righteous Judge (2 Timothy 4:8)? Does it convey that our Heavenly Father is trustworthy?

"What is the chief end of man?" Many of us know that question, and the answer to it, from the Westminster Shorter Catechism[14]. "Man's chief end is to glorify God, and to enjoy him forever." So those five reasons really channel into this one grand reason. Our meekness shows off, or glorifies, our meek and lowly Lord Jesus.

When we yield our rights to fallen people and entrust our wrongs to an unseen God, the world can't help but take a second look. Because a meek response to hard people and tough circumstances is *other*-worldly. It's totally supernatural. Meek people stand out. Meekness is so other-worldly, and requires such supernatural strength, that when we put it on, the world can't help but do a double take. Our meekness glorifies our Lord Jesus.

That is why meekness matters.

FOR FURTHER REFLECTION:

1. Of all the adjectives our Lord could have chosen to self-identify, Jesus Christ chose "humble" and "meek." As you think of the life of Jesus, where do you see his meekness?

2. *Fresh joy, abundant peace, and divine guidance* are three of the rewards promised to the meek. Which of these is most motivating for you? How do you think each might be related to being meek?

3. Jack the Kicker was a wild pony. He was not used to human touch, not broken for riding, not useful and not meek. How does Jack explain the "usefulness" piece of meekness and its importance?

4. Most of us know that certain colors look good on us. But have you ever thought of certain virtues "looking good" on you? How would you "clothe yourself with meekness?" What would it look like to those around you if you were to wear meekness?

5. Discuss Matthew Henry's observation that "our meekness is more obvious than our love for God or our faith in Christ." Whose meekness has impressed you? What actions or attitudes made his or her meekness obvious to you?

6. Now think for a minute of the opposite. Psalm 149:4 says, "For the LORD...will beautify the meek with salvation." Can you think of a time when your own lack of meekness was like wearing clashing clothes and not very beautiful? What did that look like to others around you?

7. In Part III, we will examine 8 actionable steps we can take to become more meek. But as you consider these five reasons meekness matters, which one resonates most? Why?

PRAYER OF RESPONSE

Dear Meek and Lowly Lord Jesus, help me to live as you lived in this world, to do what you would do, to walk in love and meekness, so that the world will see you through me. Help me to be responsive to your voice and yield to your hand so that I will be more useful to you. For your glory I pray,

Amen.

4 - Meekness Rests On Providence

Providence is wiser than you, and you may be confident it has suited all things better to your eternal good than you could had you been left to your own option.

—*John Flavel*[1]

But I trust in you, O LORD; I say, "You are my God." My times are in your hands.

—*Psalm 31:14-15*

My times are in your hands. Have you ever prayed that? I have. But while I would have said ten years ago "my times are in God's hands," I definitely did not *rest* in them. Looking back, I see that I often resisted God's hand. Especially when I could pin my trials on a person. I struggled to overlook, forbear, and forgive. I struggled to overcome evil with good. I struggled to speak the truth with love. I knew that God disciplines those he loves (Hebrews 12:6), but I failed to see that sometimes God's discipline comes from the hand of other sinful humans. In short, I was not meek.

Paul Tripp[3] speaks the perfect words to my un-meek predicament,

> *Our problem is that we tend to be unfaithful to his holy agenda and get kidnapped by our plans for us and our dreams for our lives. The trials in our lives exist not because he has forgotten us, but because he remembers us and is changing us by his grace. When you remember that, you can have joy in the middle of what is uncomfortable.*

Remember the Latin word for meekness, *mansuetus*—used to the hand? The meek have trained themselves by constant use to rest in God's hand, not just to refuse to resist it. They are *used* to it. As Charles Spurgeon[4] teaches, "If my times are in God's hand, no man can do me harm unless God permits." Meekness then rests in the sure knowledge that our interests are safe in the highest keeping.

Psalm 31:15's time-hand link is the affirmation of one who is hard-pressed and rests because he knows himself to be under the fatherly care of the Almighty God. This truth is for every believer. "Since our times are in God's hands," Alistair Begg[5] concludes, "we are not trapped in the grip of blind forces. We are not trapped in a cage marked fate. We are not adrift on a boat marked chance." Rather, we are active learners in the school of providence.

The soft pillow of providence on which we rest our heads no doubt carries the words—your times are in his hand. This is how the meek *enjoy great peace*. Is it possible to sleep like that? To rest on this pillow?

> The Lord our God never undertakes what he will not complete. "My times are in your hand," and therefore the end will be glorious. My Lord, if my times were in my own hand, they would prove a failure; but since they are in your hand, you will not fail, nor shall I.
>
> —C.H. Spurgeon[2]

A LOVE AFFAIR WITH PROVIDENCE

The blind hymn writer Fanny Crosby[6] had a love affair with providence. When she became sick as an infant, the family doctor was away. Another man—pretending to be a doctor—treated her with a prescription of hot poultices applied to her eyes. She recovered from the illness but was left blind. Decades later, a well-meaning preacher reportedly told her, "I think it is a great pity that the Master did not give you sight when he showered so many other gifts upon you."

Fanny had heard this sort of comment before and gave this reply. "Do you know that if at birth I had been able to make one petition, it would have been that I was born blind?" said the poet, who had been able to see only for her first six weeks of life. "Because when I get to heaven, the first face that shall ever gladden my sight will be that of my Savior."

The longer I study meekness, the more I see that in every meek action, or *inaction*, and from every meek man or woman there is a common thread. There lies a single underlying, rock-bottom belief. It is this: the meek all have a heightened sense of God's sovereignty. They delight in providence.

In fact, author Jerry Bridges[7] described meekness simply as, "An enlightened awareness of the sovereignty of God." Knowing that God is fully in control is central to theologian Sinclair Ferguson's[8] comprehensive definition of meekness. Meekness, he writes,

> *is an attitude toward God and man reflected in our response toward what God does and what man does. Meekness toward God is a spirit of submission to all of God's dealings toward us in the settled conviction that he is graciously, wisely, sovereignly working all things out for his glory and our good. Meekness toward men means bearing patiently with the words and actions of others and dealing gently with their failings, with the twin convictions that God is in control and that we have no claim for any better than the worst of our enemies.*

Meekness flows from faith that God is in control, especially in our trials; and therefore, we don't have to be. But it's even more than that. The meek lean into providence. As John wrote, "they know and rely on the love God has for them" (1 John 4:16). Meekness grows when we lean into providence, when we *trust* and *rely* on it.

We may glibly speak of providence. But what exactly *is* God's providence?

The Heidelberg Catechism[9], a series of 129 questions and answers dating to 1563, addresses providence in Q&A 27. Please stick with me here. I promise it's not as dry as it sounds.

<u>Question:</u> What do you understand by the providence of God?

<u>Answer:</u> *The almighty, ever present power of God, whereby, as it were, by his hand, he still upholds heaven and earth with all creatures and so governs them that herbs and grass, rain and drought, fruitful and barren years, meat and drink, health and sickness, riches and poverty, indeed, all things come not by chance, but by his fatherly hand.*

The doctrine of providence is much more personal than simple sovereignty. We can think of it as sovereignty guided by wise, loving purposes. The meek have a heightened awareness of providence. But the meek aren't just aware of providence. They trust that God is guiding all the events of the world including those difficult events in their personal lives with wisdom and love. They have internalized Psalm 31:15—*My times are in his hand*. The meek believe that God is always exercising sovereign, loving control and fatherly protective care over all the events of his children's lives. Even when it doesn't *feel* like it. They walk by faith not by feelings.

But how do they make sense of the fact that not only the pleasant things but also the hard things like poverty or persecution, cancer and car accidents come to them through God's "fatherly hand?"

They may not know these words from the Heidelberg Catechism[10], but if they did, they'd find comfort here:

> *We can be patient when things go against us, thankful when things go well, and for the future we can have good confidence in our faithful God and Father that nothing in creation can separate us from his love. For all creatures are so completely in God's hand that without his will they can neither move nor be moved.*

In other words, the meek don't just know that "God is in control." They *rest* in that knowledge by trusting God's active, good will for their lives. They know that nothing can separate them from God's love (Romans 8:31). Their meekness comes from abiding in God's love (John 15:9). The Reformer John Calvin[11] drew a straight line between meekness and love for God. Loving God, he explained, allows us,

> *[T]o see his hand in everything: to own him as the governor of the world, and the director of providence, and to acknowledge his disposal in everything that takes place....If we indeed consider that our trials are from the hand of God, then we shall be disposed meekly to receive and to quietly submit to them.*

Do you see the link? We cannot be meek without leaning into providence and looking for his hand. In fact it *is* the way of meekness, and opens the door to peace and joy (Psalm 37:11, Isaiah 29:19). The meek trust God so much that if God were to hand control to them, they would refer it right back to Him. Even if that means the presence of the hard things. Even if it means broken bodies, prodigal children, failed dreams. Even if.

Maybe you noticed the word *providence* when we read these descriptions in chapter two:

- *Meekness is the easy and quiet submission of the soul to the whole will of God as He is pleased to make it known whether by His Word or by His providence.* (Matthew Henry)
- *Meekness is forged by the way in which we bow ourselves to the will of God as he reveals it in his Word and in the providences of life.* (Sinclair Ferguson)
- *Meekness is a spirit of patient submission and humility before all providences.* (John Blanchard)

The meek have a heightened awareness of and ability to submit to God's care, in whatever form it comes. They are *not* untouched by trouble, but when trials come, they don't crumble. The meek learn to say not only, "God *can* do what he will—for he is powerful, and he *will* do what he will—for he is unchangeable," but also, "*Let* him do what he will—for he is wise and good." Matthew Henry[12] adds, "Let him do what he will for he will do what is best; and therefore if God should refer the matter to me, says the meek and quiet soul, being well assured that he knows what is good for me better than I do for myself, I would refer it to him again." This is bedrock truth for the meek.

Oh to be meek like Fanny Crosby[13]! Explaining her blindness at the hands of that incompetent, imposter doctor, Crosby reportedly said, "It seemed intended by the blessed providence of God that I should be blind all my life, and I thank him for the dispensation. If perfect earthly sight were offered to me tomorrow I would not accept it. I might not have sung hymns to the praise of God if I had been distracted by the beautiful and interesting things about me." In other words, not only *can* God do what he will but *let* him do it, because he sees my own life better than I do.

Oh to have known Mary McCarthy[14]! I was drawn to her tombstone as I toured an Irish cemetery years ago. Her last name was so faded I could barely read it. But I made out that Mary died at the young age of 42. This was her epitaph, chosen by her husband John:

> *Patient and meek beneath afflictions' rod;*
> *And why, her hope and trust were in God.*

That sentiment is a far cry from the epitaph my husband and sons would select for me. But onward we grow with God, more meek. Even when I *cannot* trace God's hand, I want to choose to believe his Word and his promises, and trust his loving heart. So I find myself like the father of the sick child telling Jesus two seemingly inconsistent things: "I believe. Help my unbelief" (Mark 9:24). This is the posture of the meek. They sit at the foot of the master proclaiming their faith and still asking for more.

To display meekness like Fanny and Mary is light years away from weakness. Such responses to hard providence requires massive spiritual strength, and growing faith. Clinging like this to God's providence will help us rest; help us sleep.

Oh, yes, and how the meek can lay down their heads and rest.

WHY THE MEEK CAN SLEEP

It has everything to do with their pillow.

Do you know what I mean about needing the "right" pillow to sleep? Too many nights tossing and turning on strange too-soft and too-firm pillows have taught me how important the right pillow can be. So now when I travel, I bring my own pillow. This enables me to sleep in all sorts of beds in foreign spaces.

Sometimes though, when I put my head on that portable pillow, hopeless thoughts still swirl. Uncertainty becomes my excuse for anxiety. When anxiety comes in panicky waves of catastrophic ruminations about a loved one making foolish, costly choices, for example—I realize I need another pillow.

The Puritans[15] had a saying: "Providence is a soft pillow for anxious heads." We may be terribly anxious about the uncertainties ahead. We may not always trust our unknown futures to a known God who sees what's ahead. We might *not* pray with David (Psalm 4:8), "I will both lie down in peace, and sleep; For You alone, O LORD, make me dwell in safety." In short, we are not always meek.

But we don't lose heart. We take comfort knowing that we are in good company. Pastor Alistair Begg[16] confides,

> *Most of the occasions of my worrying, most of the occasions of my rising fears can be traced ultimately to a loss of confidence in the doctrine of providence.... I am prepared to say, "My times are in your hands," but I am not prepared to live in the light of that truth.*

While I am uncertain about what will turn up and even less certain about the direction of my loved one's heart, I claim David's prayer for my own: "But I trust in you, O LORD; I say, "You are my God." I will myself to trust with the Psalmist: "My times are in your hand" (Psalm 31:14-15).

I will both lie down and sleep in peace—I will rest on the pillow of providence.

Jesus rested on this pillow. His head was on it that night as he slept in the stern of the boat on the stormy sea. "And a great windstorm arose, and the waves beat into the boat, so that it was already filling. But He was in the stern, asleep on a pillow" (Mark 4:37-38a, New King James Version). Yes, Jesus both used a physical cushion and modeled use of the providential pillow.

It turns out to be the very same one on which we can rest our anxious heads. The pillow that helps me sleep in the midst of the storms in this house is the same pillow that Jesus lay his head upon in the storm-tossed boat. It's the same pillow we'll need all the days of our lives.

How do we *know* Jesus rested on a cushion of providence?

Let's return to Psalm 31 where David prayed, "My times are in your hand." Several verses earlier in the same psalm, he prayed, "Into your hands I commit my spirit." We don't know what else Jesus might have prayed in the storm-tossed boat, but we do know that he *did* pray David's words in the most stressful of all times, ever. On the cross.

Luke records it near the end of his Gospel (Luke 23:44-46):

> *It was now about the sixth hour, and there was darkness over the whole land until the ninth hour, while the sun's light failed. And the curtain of the temple was torn in two. Then Jesus, calling out with a loud voice, said, "Father, into your hands I commit my spirit!"* And having said he breathed his last.

The meek can only do this because they know that injuries inflicted by fellow sinners are permitted by a sovereign God who is in complete control and who uses such events to mature, purify, and form Christlike character in them. They trust that the God who sits upon the throne is a kind God. So when faced with adversity, the meek bow the knee and rest in Christ.

This is not to say they don't lament their loss and grief. God calls us to cry out to him in our grief and pain. "Trust in him at all times, O people; pour out your heart before him; God is a refuge for us" (Psalm 62:8). The Divine Author of the Bible devoted one full book to lament. Meekness does not preclude lament. Indeed, with meek Apostle Paul, we can be "sorrowful, yet always rejoicing" (2 Corinthians 6:10a).

Paradoxically while they grieve, God's providence brings peace to the hearts of the meek. When the storms come they say, "My times are in your hand." By some miracle, they grab that pillow and fall fast asleep.

FOR FURTHER REFLECTION:

1. A century ago, the English pastor Handley Moule (11) wrote, "Circumstances are the expression of God's will." What do you think that means? Can you think of situations in the Bible where we know this is true? What questions does this idea raise for you?

2. The meek believe that God is always exercising sovereign, loving control and fatherly protective care over all the events of his children's lives. This is called providence. When do you find it difficult to lean into God's providence? When do you find it easier?

3. Meekness looks deeper than the cause of hardship to find the loving hand of God. In other words, the meek realize that what comes to them from the hand of man has been permitted by God's sovereign control, filtered by His fingers of love, and will be used by God for His glory and our ultimate good. How do these verses point to God's sovereignty?

  • Daniel 4:34-35

- Daniel 7:27

- Psalm 103:19

- 1 Timothy 6:15

4. How did our Lord Jesus rest in God's providence? Refer to Mark 4:35-41 and Luke 23:44-46 to get started. Try to look through this lens of meekness as you read the Bible. What other individuals in the Bible can you see "leaning into providence"?

5. This doctrine of providence is massive and cannot be fully grasped, even in a lifetime. How can "leaning into providence" make mistreatment and trials more bearable?

6. Matthew Henry said that the meek not only say, "God *can* do what he will, and he *will* do what he will, but also, "Let him do what he will"—for he is wise and good." Is there a meaningful difference between saying "God can do whatever he will," and "let God do what he will?"

7. As I write this, I am three weeks away from a surgery to determine if a pelvic mass is cancerous. Each pang tempts me to fear, often in the quiet of night. But as the "worst-case, what-if" waves roll in, I am training myself to say, "When I am afraid, I will trust in you ….This I know, that God is for me" (Psalm 56:3,9). This is resting my head on the pillow of providence. What would it look like for *you* to rest your head on that pillow? What circumstance do you need to trust into the hands of your heavenly Father?

PRAYER OF RESPONSE

Dear Almighty, Loving Father, please help me rest in your providence. Increase my faith so that I can trust that nothing comes to me by chance but only through your wise, loving, fatherly hand. Thank you that even when the storms rage around me, I can both lie down in peace and sleep; For you alone, O LORD, make me dwell in safety.

Amen.

DIGGING DEEPER 1

Meekness Misconceptions

As if, at any time, in heaven and on the earth, Jesus stopped bearing the Spirit's fruit—Jesus was at all times fully, even in the zealous way with which He flipped the temple back on its knees, walking in meekness.

—Jackie Hill Perry[1]

Whoever is slow to anger is better than the mighty, and he who rules his spirit than he who takes a city.

—Proverbs 16:32

In my own informal survey, eight of ten friends used one of these three words to describe *meekness: Weak, timid,* or *shy. Mousy and wishy-washy* were also used. It's no surprise, then, that meekness doesn't grace many book covers. Apart from that 300-year-old title, a Google search for meekness won't yield much. Why *would* anyone want to be more meek?

Even among committed Christ-followers, we don't place a high value on meekness. It won't make the top ten, or fifty, list as a topic for a Bible study. Even in my own Christian circles, it only comes up in passing now and then because, you know, "Blessed are the meek." When was the last time one of your friends mentioned she was seeking to be more meek?

NOT NATURAL OR NICE

It's easy to see why meekness moved from a biblical virtue to a modern-day vice. Meekness is terribly misunderstood. It is *not* emotional flabbiness, lack of conviction, complacency, timidity, or cowardice. Nor is it indecisive, wishy-washy, or forever waffling about the truth. While some may associate meekness with femininity, it is neither a feminine nor a masculine virtue. Moses and Jesus (Numbers 12:3, 2 Corinthians 10:1) were the meekest people ever to walk the earth. Theologian Sinclair Ferguson[3] says that meekness "enhances manliness and adorns femininity. *All* Christians are called to meekness."

The biggest *mis*understanding about biblical meekness is that meekness equals a sort of bland, unassertive, natural "niceness." Twentieth century British pastor, Dr. Martyn Lloyd-Jones[4] sheds light on this meekness misconception.

> *There are people who seem to be born naturally nice. That is not what the Lord means when He says, 'Blessed are the meek.' That is something purely biological, the kind of thing you get in animals. One dog is nicer than another, one cat is nicer than another. That is not meekness.*

Meekness is *not* a temperament or personality type, although some temperaments are definitely more gentle than others. It cannot be limited to certain individuals, because *all* Christians are called to have it and only the Spirit of God gives it. Which means you can't exempt yourself from meekness by saying, "It's just not me. I'm a worrier by nature. I have trust issues." Or, "God gave me a take-charge, Type-A personality. It's just not in me to be meek."

Nor, on the flipside, can you assume you're already meek because you're "naturally" more go-with-the-flow, and Type-B. This misses the mark. Because meekness is a fruit of the Holy Spirit (Galatians 5:22-23), there is *always* a supernatural dimension to it.

NOT MISBEHAVING: THE MEEK GET MAD

Another misconception about meekness is that the meek don't get angry. They do. "Meekness might get mad," John Piper[5] explains, "but it doesn't have a hair-trigger. And when it does, it's more angry over wrongs committed against the glory of God than against itself." That distinction is key. The meek get angry when God is dishonored more than when they are mistreated.

We'll study the meekest man Moses in Part II, but we see this aspect of meekness when we contrast the righteous anger of Moses with the selfish anger of Jonah. Remember when Moses came down the mountain the first time with the Ten Commandments? "When he approached the camp and saw the calf and the dancing, his anger burned and he threw the tablets out of his hands, breaking them to pieces at the foot of the mountain" (Exodus 32:19). Moses saw that "the people were running wild and out of control and had become a laughingstock to their enemies" (Exodus 32:25). They had dishonored God and it made Moses mad.

Compare this to Jonah. Remember how Jonah's story ends? He had given the evil Ninevites the message to repent, and they had. But instead of rejoicing, Jonah went outside the city to pout. Then God "provided" a shady vine for him. Next God "provided" a worm to eat the vine that shaded Jonah. Enter Jonah, a meekness anti-type. Puritan Thomas Watson[6] writes, "It was an un-meek spirit in the prophet to struggle with God: 'I do well to be angry to the death!'" (Jonah 4:9). Jonah was mad not only because the people he hated had received forgiveness and grace, but because his own perceived mistreatment by God made him uncomfortable.

> We are apt to think that he, being so holy, is therefore of a severe and sour disposition against sinners, and not able to bear them. "No," says he; "I am meek; gentleness is my nature and temper.
>
> —*Thomas Goodwin*[2]

The meek *can* get good and mad. They can "be angry and sin not" (Ephesians 4:26). Puritan Matthew Henry[7] writes, "He that was a lamb in his own cause, was a lion in the cause of God; anger at sin, as sin, is very well consistent with reigning meekness." Which is to say, like Jesus.

In fact, as you study the Gospels you'll find that all three times Scripture records Jesus' anger, it was when people were trying to block the path to God. When the Pharisees put their man-made Sabbath rules before the healing of the man with the withered hand, Jesus said, "'Is it lawful to do good or to do harm on the Sabbath, to save a life or to kill?" After looking around at them *with anger*, grieved at their hardness of heart, "He said to the man, "Stretch out your hand" (Mark 3:4-5). When his disciples stopped the children from coming to him, "Jesus was angry and said to them, 'Let the children come to me, and do not stop them, because the Kingdom of God belongs to such as these'" (Mark 10:14). Can't you almost see the veins bulging in Christ's neck when he calls the Pharisees "hypocrites, blind guides" (Matthew 23:16), and a "brood of vipers"

(Matthew 23:33)? When people blocked access to God and to his mercy, as the money changers did in the temple, Jesus got good and mad.

Author Jackie Hill Perry[8] shares how this sign of Jesus transformed her notion of meekness. Reflecting on how, full of the Holy Spirit, Christ overturned the money changers' tables, she writes,

> *As if, at any time, in heaven and on the earth, Jesus stopped bearing the Spirit's fruit—Jesus was at all times fully, even in the zealous way with which He flipped the temple back on its knees, walking in meekness...In the same way, to have a quiet and gentle spirit...would not mean I had to abandon all that I am, limp along in life, silence my personality in the name of obedience, but instead it meant that I could authentically be [who] God made me, anchored in the truth and controlled by the Spirit. When led by Him, when wanting to place my rights above His honor, [meekness] would place its hand over my heart, keeping it still and settled with peace until what was worth being said or done happened in love.*

Meekness is not a personality type. To be meek is not to be passionless, tepid, weak. It is, as Perry wrote, to place our "rights" under God's honor.

But meekness is not one-dimensional. Christ's beauty is a complex glory. It is not only that of a mighty man, nor only of a gentle servant. It is the perfect blend.

THE MIGHTY-MEEK, LION-LAMB COMPLEX GLORY OF JESUS

I cherish a photo of our week-old son cradled in my husband's strong arms. The muscular arms that haul bricks and chop wood tenderly cradle a tiny, helpless baby. This is the glory of yielded strength, the beauty of contrasts, the beauty of meekness.

Meekness is beautiful, you know. "The Lord takes pleasure in His people; He will beautify the meek with salvation" (Isaiah 49:4). Matthew Henry premised his whole book, the book that launched me into my own meekness quest years ago, with this one verse: "Let your adorning be the hidden person of the heart with the imperishable beauty of a gentle [meek] and quiet spirit, which in God's sight is very precious" (1 Peter 3:4). In Part II we'll see how meekness behaves in all sorts of hard situations. But there is one word to describe how meekness looks—beautiful.

But what is it about meekness that makes it so beautiful to God the Father?

In a message on Revelation 5:1-10, where the Lion of the tribe of Judah, who is the Lamb who was slain and is alone worthy to open the sealed scroll, John Piper[9] describes this glory of contrasts. What makes Jesus stand out as absolutely unique, he says, is that his beauty "consists in the right proportion of diverse qualities." Then he offers these stirring examples:

- *we admire him for his glory, but even more because his glory is mingled with humility;*
- *we admire him for his transcendence, but even more because his transcendence is accompanied by condescension;*
- *we admire him for his justice, but even more because it is tempered with mercy;*
- *we admire him because of how worthy he was of all good, but even more because this was accompanied by an amazing patience to suffer evil;*
- *we admire him because of his sovereign dominion over the world, but even more because this dominion was clothed with a spirit of obedience and submission;*
- *we love the way he stumped the proud scribes with his wisdom, and we love it even more because he could be simple enough to like children and spend time with them;*
- *we admire him because he could still the storm, but even more because he refused to use that power to strike the Samaritans or get himself down from the cross;*
- *we admire him for his majesty, but even more because it is a majesty in meekness.*

The glory of Jesus is that of a strong man who subverts his strength to cradle the baby. It is the perfect blend and balance of diverse qualities. Contrasts in music, in painting, and in people make up this irresistible mix we see as beauty.

So it is with our meek and mighty, Lion and Lamb Lord Jesus.

But we're not Jesus. While He calls us to *learn* from him, we are *growing* to "have the mind of Christ." This side of heaven, we all fall short of His glory.

We'll look more at how we grow in Part III. But for now, know that keeping silent often takes more strength than speaking. Jesus had strength to resist every temptation (Hebrews 4:15), so we know that when he spoke and when he held his peace, he was doing the Father's will (John 5:30). We are children learning, growing more meek. Please know that God knows how challenging this is. He gives more grace.

Meekness requires, and reveals, massive inner strength and self-control. Proverbs 16:32 says, "Whoever is slow to anger is better than the mighty, and he who rules his spirit than he who takes a city." Self-controlled, humble meekness is a superpower. Strength and confidence, not weakness and insecurity, breed meekness. Kevin DeYoung[10] says, "It is being self-controlled when we are not in control."

It might look weak to the world when we yield our cause because we trust God. We might come off as powerless when we hold our peace when we're wronged. But just try to forgive and overlook or to commit your cause to God, and suddenly you'll know how much soul strength is needed.

That strength of soul is called meekness.

FOR FURTHER REFLECTION

1. Before reading Part I, how would you have described "meekness?"

2. Did you have any of the "meekness misconceptions" addressed in Part I? What were they? Why do you think meekness is so misunderstood and devalued in our world?

3. Jackie Hill Perry had an epiphany about meekness. Being meek, she realized, "would not mean I had to abandon all that I am, limp along in life, or silence my personality in the name of obedience." How does this add to your understanding of meekness?

4. Beauty "consists in the right proportion of diverse qualities." Of the bullet points describing the way Christ Jesus displayed diverse qualities, which are most beautiful to you and why?

5. Meekness, like the other fruit of the Spirit, is a mark of spiritual growth and maturity. In 2 Corinthians 10:1, Paul confronts the church, "by the meekness and gentleness of Christ." Pastor Kevin DeYoung cites this text to say, "Mature Christians are eager to be gentle but willing to be bold." How can boldness and gentleness co-exist in the meek?

6. The meek might get angry, but if they do it is because God is being dishonored not because they are being personally mistreated. Read Jonah 4 and Mark 3:1-6. Contrast Jesus' anger at "hardness of hearts" with Jonah's, "I am angry enough to die!"

7. What makes you angry? How can you discern the difference between the moments you are being a lion in God's cause or a lamb for your own?

PRAYER OF RESPONSE

Dear holy, majestic God, thank you that you are victorious "for the cause of truth and meekness and righteousness." Thank you that you are mighty in power and slow to anger. Help me to be patient with others, too, and to be quicker to defend your name and cause than my own.

Amen.

PART II

MEEK MASTERS

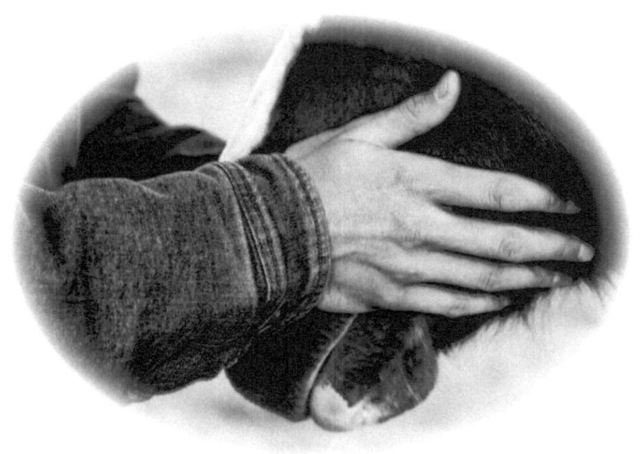

5 - Joseph: Meekness When Mistreated & Forgotten

Facebook hurt my feelings again. The caption read, "Bonfire and s'mores with friends," and the photo featured a fire, s'mores, and eight of my teen-aged son's church friends. But not my son. He had not been invited. The initial pangs at being left out were soon replaced by indignation. So unkind—didn't my friends know I'd see their post? I'm friends with all the moms she tagged.

But what does meekness do? Well, what Abigail wanted to do was post a passive-aggressive comment so they'd know how much not being invited hurt. But meekness wouldn't allow it. Satan tempted, but the Holy Spirit encouraged me to be meek. I thought of saying nothing and texting the mom, just so she'd know. But that implies entitlement and the meek receive with gratitude. The host gets to invite. It's not my prerogative to tell my friend who she should invite.

But there's more. Meekness didn't let me off that easily. I felt constrained to like the post before I left. Not in an attempt to wound one who wounded me. But as a genuine joy at the time these dear friends had together. So, with the Spirit at work in me, that's just what I did. Like. Then I got another chance to prove it when that mom and I crossed paths the next morning. I thought of mentioning my hurt. But meekness beckoned me to show self-control. So I held my tongue and smiled.

LEAN INTO PROVIDENCE

Because meek me can look past the second causes—in this case, my friend's hurtful post—to the loving hand of God that allowed me to log on to Facebook at just the right time to see first in my feed the friends minus my son around the campfire. This is looking past the "second cause" to the wise, loving hand of God. A second cause is a caused cause—*a cause through which God, the First Cause, works.* The meek recognize that the hurts and snubs, accidental or intended, may be the *exact* provocations that God is working for the good.

> The soul that has learned the blessed secret of seeing God's hand in all that concerns it cannot be a prey to fear. It looks beyond all second causes, straight into the heart and will of God and rests content because He rules.
>
> —Susannah Spurgeon[2]

In other words, the meek lean into providence. The Reformer John Calvin[3] described it clearly. To continue with the providence language we've introduced in this book, when you read "immediate source" below, think "second cause."

> *The fact that the hand of God is a great deal more involved in all that happens to us than the treatment of men is, should lead us, not to think of things as from men, but to have respect to them chiefly as from God— as ordered by his love and wisdom, even when their immediate source may be the malice or heedlessness of a fellowman. And if we indeed consider and feel that they are from the hand of God, then we [can] meekly receive and submit to them, and own that the greatest injuries received from men are justly and even kindly ordered by God.*

I hope the old language doesn't obscure that meaning. Calvin is saying that seeing God as the ultimate source of all that happens to us, even if the "immediate source" is another sinful human, summons meekness. This is what I mean by the meek "look past second causes."

Joseph awesomely modeled this core aspect of meekness when he told his brothers, "As for you, you meant evil against me, but God meant it for good"

(Genesis 50:20a). If Joseph could say those words after being sold into slavery—and what could be more hurtful than that—can't we say it for infinitely lesser offenses like insensitive remarks and unsolicited advice?

How would you respond if your siblings hated you so much that they sold you to a slave trader? How would you react if the boss for whom you had faithfully worked believed a lie about you and then had you thrown into jail? How would you feel then, if a jailmate broke a promise and as a result, you spent more years in prison?

Joseph faced exactly those circumstances. He got the wrong treatment for doing the right things. You can read the full account of his sufferings in Genesis 37-50. Joseph's is a *fortunately unfortunately* story, and it all started with two of his dreams. In both, his eleven brothers and his parents bow down to him. Joseph's brothers were jealous. They hated him for his dreams—his dreams and his special many-colored coat.

Soon the brothers get their chance. Joseph comes to them alone, wearing his favorite-son coat. "Here comes this dreamer," they say. "Let's kill him and throw him into one of the pits. Then we will say that a fierce animal has devoured him, and we will see what will become of his dreams."

Then along comes a caravan of Ishmaelites heading for Egypt (Genesis 37:5). The brothers decide to sell him as a slave for cash. They keep his colorful coat, soak it in animal blood, and let their father Jacob believe Joseph was killed by wild animals.

In Egypt, Joseph is bought by an official named Potiphar (Genesis 37:36). Joseph yields to God's "strange providence" and serves Potiphar faithfully. God is with him and he gains trust over Potiphar's household. But his responsibility is not rewarded. Instead, Potiphar's wife tries to seduce Joseph and when he flees, leaving his cloak in her hands, she gets vicious and lies about Joseph. Potiphar throws faithful, righteous Joseph in prison.

Totally unaware of God's design, Joseph again serves faithfully and, in turn, is rewarded with new responsibility. With God's wisdom, he interprets the dreams of Pharaoh's butler and baker, who just so happened to be imprisoned with Joseph. The butler is released, but forgets to mention Joseph, which is unfortunate. But at just the right moment, he remembers—at the time appointed by God, when Pharaoh was desperate to have his own dreams explained. So Joseph is released from prison and explains the dreams. The interpretations make sense to Pharaoh, and he makes Joseph vice-president of Egypt. "You shall be over my house," Pharaoh says (Genesis 41:40), "and all my people shall order themselves as you command. Only as regards the throne will I be greater than you."

Then, as predicted, seven years of famine follow seven years of plenty. But Joseph had gathered huge grain reserves during the seven good years. The drought hits Jacob's family hard. In desperation, Joseph's brothers are forced to seek grain in Egypt. Twenty-two years had gone by since the brothers had sold the 17-year-old Joseph (Genesis 37:2, 41:46, 53; 45:6). They don't recognize him until he reveals himself, and when he does, it is *not* as a victim.

While Scripture doesn't use the word "meek" to describe him, at every turn, what is recorded of him *is* meek. He did not take revenge. He neither wallowed in self-pity when he was mistreated nor did he punish his brothers. In situations he did not choose and in a foreign land, he was faithful to Potiphar, faithful to the jailer, and faithful to Pharoah.

NOT MERELY "ALLOWED" BUT MEANT BY GOD FOR GOOD

Joseph rejected bitterness against those who had wronged him and, in meekness, chose instead to see them, not as first causes, but as instruments in God's hand. He interpreted his mistreatment by sinful people not only as *allowed*, but a step further, as *intended* and *meant* by God for good. Joseph refused to believe his years in slavery were a divine accident that God opted to redeem. Thus, he refused to see himself as a victim and responded to suffering in faith and with meekness. As he did, God used him not only to save his betrayers' lives, but to fulfill the promise he had given to Joseph's great-grandfather Abraham in Genesis 15:13-14,

> *Know for certain that your offspring will be sojourners in a land that is not theirs and will be servants there, and they will be afflicted for four hundred years.*

The all-knowing God of the universe *knew* this would happen. But more, God *intended* it. He *meant* it. Joseph's sale into Egyptian slavery was no accident. To make sure we don't miss this key point in Genesis, the Psalmist makes it plain (Psalm 105:16-17): "When he summoned a famine on the land and broke all supply of bread, he had sent a man ahead of them, Joseph, who was sold as a slave." Do you see it? *God* summoned a famine and broke the bread supply and sent Joseph ahead. Nothing about these events was random. Not for a split second was the Lord caught off guard.

But after their father Jacob died, Joseph's brothers justifiably feared for their lives. As second in command of Egypt, Joseph had the authority to punish them.

A normal human being would take vengeance. But Joseph does not do the normal, natural thing. By faith, he does something supernatural.

Joseph leans into providence. In Genesis 50:19-21 Joseph shows us the perfect example of meekness, of power under control, when he assures his brothers:

> *"Don't be afraid. Am I in the place of God? As for you, you meant to harm me, but God intended it for a good purpose, so he could preserve the lives of many people, as you can see this day. So now, don't be afraid. I will provide for you and your little children." Then he consoled them and spoke kindly to them.*

If the key to meekness is trusting that God's fatherly wisdom is behind everything that happens to us, then the key to expressing that meekness toward others is trusting that we are not in the place of God. When Joseph asks, "Am I in the place of God?" he reveals his belief that he did not have the right to take vengeance on them despite their horrific actions. Meek Joseph knew that right belonged to God.

Instead, Joseph chose to bless them, to overcome evil with good. This is exactly what Paul taught in Romans 12:19, 21:

> *Do not avenge yourselves, dear friends, but give place to God's wrath, for it is written, "Vengeance is mine, I will repay," says the Lord ...Do not be overcome by evil, but overcome evil with good.*

Jesus Christ, the King of meekness, modeled this perfectly. "When he was maligned, he did not answer back; when he suffered, he threatened no retaliation, but committed himself to God who judges justly" (1 Peter 2:23). The meek follow Jesus like this.

MEEKNESS "SEES NO SECOND CAUSES"

I never knew Janet[4] but I wish I would have. She was surely a meek master. Janet looked straight through second causes to see God's loving, ruling hand working out his good designs.

> *She delighted in seeing her plan upset by unexpected events, saying that it gave her great comfort, and that she looked on such things as an assurance that God was watching over her stewardship, was securing the accomplishment of His will, and working out His own designs. Whether she traced the secondary causes to the prayer of a child, to the imperfection of an individual, to obstacles arising from misunderstandings, or to interference of outside agencies, she was*

> *joyfully and graciously ready to recognize the indication of God's ruling hand, and to allow herself to be guided by it.*

Did you catch this: she "joyfully and graciously" recognized obstacles to her plans as "the indication of God's ruling hand"? In other words, "meekness sees no second causes" means that we receive interruptions, and "unexpected events" not as a sign that God is unloving or out of control, but that he is *working out* his good plans. This is counter-cultural and counter human wisdom. Only the meek, in Christ, can do this.

Since God is in control, the meek don't feel the need to be. They trust that God is *always* at work in his world, at every second working out his plans and fulfilling his good purposes (Job 42:2, Isaiah 46:10). The meek trust that God will get the last word and that he will always do right (Psalm 33:10-11, Genesis 18:25). Because Joseph was meek, he did not resent adversity.

The meek, says Vine's Bible Dictionary, "accept everything as being the effect of God's wise and loving purpose for them so that they accept injuries from men also, knowing that these are permitted by God for their ultimate good." In other words, even though it might be an intentional wrong of a mean person (someone bashed in your mailbox or stole your wallet), an unintentional failure of a forgetful person (a friend stood you up for coffee or made a hurtful comment) or a random act of nature (a foot of water in your basement or hail damage to your new car), you look further beyond the wrongs to the God who allowed them. We respond, not with resentment and rage, but with humility and grace.

If God allows me to see a certain Facebook post or to catch a cold or miss a flight, I must trust that they will be used for good even if I don't see that good in the moment, or even in this lifetime.

These three images have helped me to receive with meekness the trials that come my way. We can choose to view the irritations and hard situations as:

1. **God's heavenly sandpaper.** Yes, it will feel abrasive. People will rub us wrong, but the meek don't chafe at the coarsest grit.

2. **A God-sent wave**[5]. The meek learn to kiss the wave that throws us up against the Rock of Ages.

3. **God's gymnasium. Christ is our trainer.** The meek listen to the instructor, do the exercises, and take the training.

The meek grow to know, as John Blanchard[6] explains, that "God has the right to do whatever he chooses to do, whenever he chooses to do it, with whomever he chooses to do it, in whatever way he chooses to do it, and for whatever purpose he chooses to do it."

If I mean to be meek, I must accept that whatever God allows to happen becomes for me his will at that moment. Perhaps it was someone else's sinful action, but if God allows it to affect me he intends it for my sanctification and good. Receiving it with meekness makes me look more like Jesus and pleases God. "Those please God who are pleased with him," Matthew Henry noted[7] "and with all he does, whether immediately by his own hand, or mediately by the agency of provoking, injurious man."

The key to meekness is learning to look through tough circumstances and difficult people to God's goodness; to trust his mighty hand is working in all things. Seeing God's hand in our hardships and meekness are inextricably linked.

Theologian and author John Piper[8] wrote a book with a provocative title, *Spectacular Sins*. He dedicated the book to Joseph. Here he explains why,

> *The point of the story emerges after poor Joseph has been mistreated by the slaveholders, lied about by Potiphar's wife, refused to be remembered by the cupbearer when he was sent back to the king, and his life was miserable for all those years. All the while he was being loved and used by God for the rescue of the people of God. So Joseph—probably more extensively in the Bible than any other character—is one whose story is to make the point, "You meant it for evil, but God meant it for good."*

Not merely *used* for good but *meant* for good. More and more the meek rest in, and not merely endure, the thought that God knows exactly what they need to smooth off their rough edges and that his heavenly sandpaper includes people who irritate, hurt, and mistreat them. The meek know that God is using the situation to impact more people than them alone, just as God meant the brothers' sin to save not only their lives but the lives of his people Israel.

This is how trials are turned to triumphs, how headstrong spirits are tamed, and how our untamed power is brought under control. Refusing to focus on second causes and choosing to trust God's invisible, guiding hand forges meekness.

When, with Joseph, we choose to see the provoking people in our lives not as *obstacles* to our good, but as *instruments* in God's hand for a greater good than we can see—this, too, is meek.

FOR FURTHER REFLECTION:

1. Why are some people able to look past the wrongs done to them to the God who allowed those wrongs and respond, not with resentment and rage, but with humility and grace? What truths about God can help us live like this?

2. Joseph's life is an amazing tale of how the sinful hand of man was working the perfect will of God. How did Joseph model looking past a wrong inflicted on him by sinful people to God's loving, fatherly hand? How did that keep him from seeing himself as a victim?

3. How do you respond: When a friend or spouse makes an insensitive comment about you or you realize you got ripped off or someone breaks a tool they borrowed from you? How do you think a meek response would look?

4. Why is it so difficult to leave justice with God when we are hurt? Should we, at times, defend ourselves? If so, when? See Paul's example in Acts 22:23-30.

5. Which of the three illustrations for accepting difficult people and hard circumstances do you like best: divine sandpaper, a heaven-sent wave, or God's gymnasium? Why?

6. Read Romans 12:19-21 and Genesis 50:19-21. How are they alike? How do both texts express meekness?

7. In Genesis 45:5, Joseph displays massive meekness in these words, "Do not be distressed or angry with yourselves because you sold me here, for God sent me before you to preserve life." With whom does God want you to show forgiveness and mercy?

PRAYER OF RESPONSE

Dear God in Heaven, I believe that you govern all things for your glory and our good. Please help me believe like Joseph that you are not caught off guard when others hurt or mistreat me and that you mean all things for good, even when they don't feel good. Please increase my faith. For Jesus' sake,

Amen.

6 - Moses: Meekness When Opposed & Told No

Do God's ways ever seem extreme? Do you second-guess how God doles out discipline? Do you ever think that sometimes divine judgment seems far too severe for the sin?

When I read this, I did. It explains how God dealt with his servant Moses because he struck a rock.

> *Take the staff, and assemble the congregation, you and Aaron your brother, and tell the rock before their eyes to yield its water. So you shall bring water out of the rock for them… And Moses lifted up his hand and struck the rock with his staff twice, and water came out abundantly, and the congregation drank, and their livestock. And the Lord said to Moses and Aaron, "Because you did not believe in me, to uphold me as holy in the eyes of the people of Israel, therefore you shall not bring this assembly into the land that I have given them.* (Numbers 20:8, 11-12)

Moses had been told to strike a rock before (Exodus 17:1-7). He did and water gushed from the rock. So what's the big deal now? What's the difference between talking to and striking rocks? And what would drive Moses to lash out this way?

Was he angry? Frustrated? Rebellious? Frustration and anger seem like front runners. God himself had called his own people *rebels* (Numbers 17:10). Psalm 106 tells us that the people "sorely provoked Moses." One commentary says, "It went badly with Moses on their account, for they made his spirit bitter, and he spoke rashly with his lips." Can we really blame him for lashing out if that's why he struck rather than spoke?

> Doesn't God often take advantage of the hardest things that come to us, using them to visit our souls with His Spirit's comfort, leading us through them into the glory of His Word, making us taste the love He has had for us from before the world began? Think about these things—and then let us learn to kiss the rod that disciplines us.
>
> —John Bunyan[2]

Please don't miss God's mercy in his judgment. Despite the people's grumbling, and despite the disobedience of Moses, God gave water abundantly to his rebel people and their animals.

The consequences help us notice what God was doing. What Moses couldn't see. What only God can see. Why trust is at the heart of meekness. Still came the consequence: "Because you did not believe in Me, to uphold me as holy in the eyes of the people of Israel, therefore you shall not bring this assembly into the land that I have given them" (Numbers 20:12).

God kept Moses out of the Promised Land because he did not believe the Lord or uphold the Lord as holy.

Seems extreme, doesn't it? Moses was God's servant, his choice among all the men on earth to lead his people out of slavery. The "Man of God"—as Psalm 90 calls him—brought the Israelites out of Egypt through the sea and for 40 years led them through the wilderness. We would expect that Moses would be the one to finally bring them into the Promised Land.

But he was not.

WHEN GOD BLAMED HIS MEEKEST MAN

That is because God *did* blame Moses. He *did* find fault in Moses and *did* hold him responsible. That's what blame means. Numbers 20:12 makes that plain: "Because you did not believe in me, to uphold me as holy in the eyes of the people of Israel, therefore you shall not bring this assembly into the land that I have given them." The offense was serious enough in God's eyes to ban Moses from leading Israel into Canaan—Moses, "the meekest man."

There is comfort here or those who struggle in this area. We are in good company. Bible scholars[3] agree that it seems "excessively harsh." We'll get back to that, but first let's consider another key reason God gave Moses "the meekest man" moniker.

Whether Moses or another scribe added it, the Holy Spirit wanted us to know that Moses *was* the meekest man on earth. That is recorded in Numbers 12. The immediate context is his own brother and sister's complaints against him.

> *Miriam and Aaron spoke against Moses because of the Cushite woman whom he had married, for he had married a Cushite woman. And they said, "Has the Lord indeed spoken only through Moses? Has he not spoken through us also?" And the Lord heard it. Now the man Moses was very meek, more than all people who were on the face of the earth.* (Numbers 12:1-3)

Notice that Moses did not resent the words spoken against him, or complain about it to God. But God took note. Pastor Robert Rayburn[4] counsels, "The more silent we are in our own cause, the more God is engaged to plead it. The accused innocent needs to say little if he knows the judge himself will be his advocate." This was surely true for Moses. He was so meek that he did not offer a single word of defense when opposed.

He didn't have to because "the Lord came down" and spoke to Aaron and Miriam. "'With him I speak mouth to mouth, clearly, and not in riddles, and he beholds the form of the LORD. Why then were you not afraid to speak against my servant Moses?' And the anger of the LORD was kindled against them" (Numbers 12:7-9). After all, he hand-picked Moses to lead his people.

Here we see the principle that the lion in God's cause should be a lamb in his own. When the complaint was against him personally, Moses remained silent. He left his vindication to God, even as Christ the Son did. In 1 Peter 2:23, Peter offers Jesus as our example. "When they hurled their insults at him, he did not retaliate; when he suffered, he made no threats. Instead he entrusted himself to him who judges justly."

I don't know about you, but left to myself I morph into a roaring lion when I am mistreated or misunderstood. Christ left us this example, that we should follow in his footsteps. This is hard. These are supernaturally trod steps. It's impossible to walk like this on my own. Into lion land, but for the grace of God go I. In Moses and in the Lord Jesus, we see how the meek act when they are opposed.

We find another key meekness marker in Moses' response to God's discipline. Let's go back to the moment he struck the rock. On the surface it sounds like the punishment was too severe for the crime. Like banning dessert for a year because your five-year-old stole a cookie, or denying a week at camp for a minute of sassy talk.

Trust is at the heart of meekness. Specifically, trusting the righteous Judge is at the core. Like Abraham said, "Surely the Judge of the earth will do right" (Genesis 18:25). My first reaction to this incident with Moses striking the rock is not very trusting, not very meek. Why *was* God so hard on Moses?

Scripture gives us a clear answer. Because instead of doing what God said—"Speak to the rock, and water will gush out" (Numbers 20:8)—Moses dishonored God and disobeyed. "He lifted up his hand and struck the rock with his staff twice and water came out abundantly, and the congregation drank, and their livestock" (Numbers 20:11).

It seems God was less concerned about quenching the physical thirst of the Israelites and more concerned with a display of his power. A power that would lead many to trust in the ultimate thing. The Rock that would bring forth living water that would leave none thirsty again would be the Word made flesh. The ultimate Judge knew all that. But Moses was called to trust when he did not know what God was up to.

DISBELIEF AND DISOBEDIENCE: PARTNERS IN CRIME

Disbelief and disobedience often go hand-in-hand. They did for the Israelites in the desert (see Hebrews 4:1-11) and they do for us today. "Take heed, brothers, lest there be in you an evil, unbelieving heart, that turns away from the living God" (Hebrews 3:12). Moses overtly disobeyed God (Numbers 20:8,11). When commanded, he chose his way. Moses did not uphold God as holy in the eyes of the people. That was sin.

Here's the deeper layer that helps me understand why this particular sin, striking the rock twice, was so offensive to God. We don't always get to know why. Don't miss this: the God of the universe does not owe us an explanation. In this particular case however, we get a glimpse into what God was up to. I want us to remember this story when we feel his chastening hand and do not understand why. This is meat for the meek.

After reading a dozen commentaries on Numbers 20, every Bible scholar drove this one particular point home:

When Moses struck the rock, he "broke the type."

Type? What exactly is a type? It's a picture of something that is to come. It's a person or thing that has a meaning that extends past itself to teach us about Christ.

God had given very specific directions to Moses for building the tabernacle, the portable sanctuary for God. "See that you make everything according to the pattern shown to you on the mountain" (Exodus 25:9,40; Exodus 40:16-33, Hebrews 8:5; 9:23). It went like this, "Moses did as the LORD had commanded him." The curtains, veil, lampstand, altar, basin and table were all to be just as God had commanded. Meekness, remember, submits to God's word. In all these, the meekest man Moses obeyed God to a T.

And that was good because all those things were types. Moses didn't understand that they pointed to something else, or how. But they did. He obeyed without knowing that the altar says our sin must be dealt with by sacrifice. The veil blocked the way between sinful man and the presence of God in the Holy of Holies. Each furnishing in the tabernacle pointed beyond itself to a spiritual reality. Moses obeyed without knowing any of that. He believed the great I Am without explanation. He obeyed.

Back to the rock. The rock was a type too. Scripture is clear: "They drank from the spiritual Rock that followed them, and the Rock was Christ" (1 Corinthians 10:4b).

So when God barred his meekest man Moses from entering the Promised Land, it wasn't simply for striking a rock.

It was for striking **the** Rock.

STRUCK ONLY ONCE

God *had* commanded Moses to strike the Rock once before (Exodus 17:6) but he was not to strike again. Why? The reason is critical. Because the Rock represents God's beloved Son, the Suffering Servant, our Jesus Christ. Christ was struck once. He died once, never to die again. That truth is repeated again and again so we won't miss it.

- Hebrews 9:28, "So Christ was offered **once** to bear the sins of many."
- Hebrews 10:10, "[W]e are sanctified through the offering of the body of Jesus Christ **once** for all."
- Hebrews 10:12, "But Christ offered for all time a **single** sacrifice for sins…"
- 1 Peter 3:18, "For Christ also suffered **once** for sins, the just for the unjust."

Christ was struck for us once and for all. Our Prince of Glory died only once on that wondrous cross.

That type is most precious to God.

DOES GOD STILL DISCIPLINE HIS CHILDREN?

Last week I sat around a table with several sisters in Christ. When the subject of suffering came up, one quickly said, "Well, I know suffering can't be from God because God doesn't punish his people."

If by punishment she meant God's holy wrath—his pay-back punishment for sin, rather than his corrective discipline and pruning of those he loves—she is definitely right.

God disciplines those he loves. Discipline isn't comfortable. Or pleasant. But it is loving. We learn in Hebrews "that for the moment all discipline seems painful rather than pleasant" (Hebrews 12:5-11). God's love includes discipline, which means we experience pain. Even though our loving Father forgives us completely when we confess, as far as east from west, in this life, sin's consequences remain.

John Piper's description[5] clarifies the meaning of this fatherly discipline,

> *There is an infinite difference between the painful things that come into our lives and discipline us—designed for our good that we may share God's holiness as loved children—and that terrible experience of pure retribution where we simply bear what we deserve and experience God's justice forever.*

I think the lady at my table did what many of us do. She conflated two ideas. She joined the false idea that God's children will never suffer on earth because of their sin with the glorious truth that God's children will never, here or hereafter, suffer the eternal wrath of God.

Jesus took that wrath. He was struck by it for our sins, once and for all. "He bore *our* sins in His body on the tree" (1 Peter 2:24). The record of *our* debt was nailed to the cross (Colossians 2:15). We bear it no more. "There is therefore now no condemnation for those who are in Christ Jesus" (Romans 8:1). Game, set, match. Hallelujah, amen!

This incident with Moses shows us in heart-achingly vivid color that sin has a ripple effect. It still has consequences for someone. This side of glory, God, in his mercy, decides when we must experience consequences from our sin. In Deuteronomy 3:23-29. Like all Scripture, this one was written for our instruction so that we might have hope (Romans 15:4).

The Child's Story Bible[6] is succinct.

> *This was a bitter disappointment to Moses. He begged God to let him cross the river so that he, too, could see the longed-for promised land. God did not give Moses what he asked for. "Be satisfied with what I have decided," God said to him. "Do not speak about this anymore. Climb this mountain, and I will show you the land. Then you are to die here on this mountain. For you are not to cross the river." (Deuteronomy 3:26)*

Even for God's blood-bought children, sin still has consequences in this life. The Lord, in his mercy, knows when and how to discipline those he loves.

The meek may beg for understanding. They may cry out to God. They may ask for relief. For this cup to pass. This is what Moses did. God said *No. No,* he could not enter the Promised Land. So Moses went boldly to God, as a man to his friend, and asked if he could be allowed in. God's no was final. As the meek mature, they learn to recognize when no when is the final answer. Once that becomes clear, they don't resist and they don't resent. They trust. They grow.

But until then, that *doesn't* mean they don't ask for relief. This is what Paul did. He asked for the thorn in his flesh to be removed. Three times he asked and three times God said *No.* While physical relief did not come, understanding did.

> *But he said to me, "My grace is sufficient for you, for my power is made perfect in weakness." Therefore I will boast all the more gladly of my weaknesses, so that the power of Christ may rest upon me. For the sake of Christ, then, I am content with weaknesses, insults, hardships, persecutions, and calamities. For when I am weak, then I am strong. (2 Corinthians 12:9-10)*

Paul gives us a stunning picture of meekness in the facing of God's no–holding no with an unresistant, unresentful, grateful heart. On the surface, asking boldly doesn't seem meek. Meekness sounds weak, timid, and shy. But remember how we've defined meekness: submission to divine control, both directly and as God allows provoking people and circumstances in our lives.

Being denied is provoking. No one likes to be told no. Submitting to someone else's control is meek. Yielding my will to another's control takes tremendous inner strength, which is why meekness like we saw earlier with Jack, grandpa's kicking pony, is strength under control.

Why are courageous requests and the ability to accept NO keys to meekness? Why is "go bold and take no" a meek mark?

When we aren't *sure* of God's will, when we don't sense his steering or pull on the reins, we can kick meekness down the road. But, please follow me here, if meekness is submitting to God's will, and if his will couldn't be more clear than when he answers a request with *no*, then our going bold with our requests forces the issue of meekness. It forces us to see our need for meekness. The gift of meekness.

Which is *exactly* what Moses did. The meekest man made a bold request: *May I please go into the Promised Land?* And his request was unequivocally denied by God. *No. You shall not cross over the Jordan and go into it.*

But that is not the end of the story. Even though God disciplined Moses for his sin, God's meekest man Moses was precious to God. Yes, he was disciplined, but he was still highly favored and beloved. When the Rock, who was Christ, walked this earth and was transfigured on the mountain (Matthew 17:1-3) along with the great prophet Elijah, Moses appeared with him in his glory. In the way only God can work, Moses ultimately got the deep desire of his heart—to enter the Promised Land. He appeared with Jesus in the Promised Land.

When, with the meekest man Moses, we trust God to defend us when we are opposed and go boldly to God, willing to take his *no*—this, too, is meek.

FOR FURTHER REFLECTION:

1. Have you ever thought that sometimes God's discipline seems severe? How did studying the story of Moses striking the rock in Numbers 20 affect you?

2. Moses was called the meekest man in Numbers 12:3, in the context of his bearing the jealousy and opposition from his brother and sister. Have you ever had opposition from others for doing the right thing? How did you respond?

3. In Luke 6:27-28, "But to you who are listening I say: 'Love your enemies, do good to those who hate you, bless those who curse you, pray for those who mistreat you.'" Have you ever prayed for those who hurt or mistreat you? What effect did that have on you?

4. How would you respond to someone who said God doesn't discipline his children? Use Hebrews 12:4-12 in your answer. What is the purpose of discipline?

5. Do you think it is possible to become meek without facing adversity? Explain your answer.

6. How does making a bold request, of a person or of God, force the issue of meekness?

7. How did Moses respond to being told no? How did Paul respond to having his request rejected by God? See 2 Corinthians 12:8-10. Why do you think our reaction to "no" can be a good indicator of our meekness? How could you grow in meekness, either by asking bold requests or gracefully receiving no?

PRAYER OF RESPONSE

Lord, You have been our dwelling place in all generations. From everlasting to everlasting you are God. Help me to come boldly to you with requests and to trust that when you say "no," it is for my best. Thank you that you promise the peaceful fruit of righteousness to those trained by discipline. I want to be tamed and trained, for the glory of Jesus,

Amen.

7 - David: Meekness When Disciplined & Provoked

> Let us pray unto God that we may see His hand in every affliction and say, as David does, "Oh, Lord, Your rod and Your staff—they comfort me!"
>
> —*Thomas Watson*[1]

> And have you forgotten the exhortation that addresses you as sons? My son, do not regard lightly the discipline of the Lord, nor be weary when reproved by him. For the Lord disciplines the one he loves, and chastises every son whom he receives.
>
> —*Hebrews 12:5-6*

What do you know about David? I mean, beyond slaying Goliath and sleeping with Bathsheba?

Did you know that God said, "I have found in David the son of Jesse a man after my heart…" (Acts 13:22)?

Why *did* David receive such high praise?

WHAT *WAS* IT ABOUT DAVID?

One can only imagine the many reasons he received such an honor. He waited patiently for the LORD (Psalm 40:1), worshiped with his whole heart (Psalm 86:12), fearlessly fought for God's glory (1 Samuel 17:45), and persistently sought the presence of the LORD (2 Samuel 21:1).

But what about the way David accepted God's dealings with him? Nineteenth century Scottish preacher Alexander MacLaren[3] described meekness as "the accepting of His dealings, of whatever complexion they are, and however they may tear or desolate our hearts, without murmuring, without sulking, without rebellion or resistance. Meekness toward God is, first, patient endurance of his will." By that standard, David was a meek man. From the Bathsheba incident, to Shimei's cursing and then his foolish census decision (2 Samuel 11, 1 Chronicles 16 and 21), David patiently endured God's will.

David was a man after God's heart because he received the "rod" of God's discipline with meekness. Whether it came directly from a holy God or through the second cause of a sinful man, David received it as from the hand of God who intended his good. He neither "made light" of the Lord's discipline nor did he "lose heart" at his rebuke (Hebrews 12:5b). In other words, he neither blew off corrections nor wallowed in self-pity's muck.

> He that is down needs fear no fall, he that is low, no pride;
>
> he that is humble ever shall have God to be his guide.
>
> —John Bunyan[2]

Like Moses, David knew that the presence of consequences did not signal the absence of God's love. Centuries before God breathed it out, David knew the truth of Hebrews 12:6, that "the Lord disciplines the one he loves." We can hear it in Psalm 141:5 when he boldly proclaims: "[L]et a righteous man strike me—it is a kindness; let him rebuke me—it is oil for my head; let my head not refuse it."

Let's start with a quick review. Most are familiar with David's adultery with Bathsheba, the cover-up, and the wartime murder of her husband Uriah. The child conceived is born. To our knowledge, David has not repented. So the LORD sends the prophet Nathan to tell David a story—an analogy.

We read Nathan's parallel to David's transgression in 2 Samuel 12:2-4. He describes a rich man with very many flocks and herds, and a poor man with "nothing but one little ewe lamb." That lamb was like a prized pet that even "used to eat of his morsel and drink from his cup and lie in his arms, and it was like a daughter to him." But when a leg was needed to feed a traveling guest, the rich man refused to take from his own large flock and took the poor man's lamb.

When the slaughter of the poor man's precious lamb arouses King David's anger, Nathan drops the bomb: "You are the man!" David gets it. He's heartbroken and immediately confesses, "I have sinned against the LORD." Then, just as

Nathan had foretold, the child conceived with Bathsheba gets sick. David humbles himself with fasting and prayer, but after seven days the child dies.

What happens next is surprising.

> *Then David got up from the ground. After he had washed, put on lotions and changed his clothes, he went into the house of the Lord and worshiped. Then he went to his own house, and at his request they served him food, and he ate.*
>
> *His attendants asked him, "Why are you acting this way? While the child was alive, you fasted and wept, but now that the child is dead, you get up and eat!"*
>
> *He answered, "While the child was still alive, I fasted and wept. I thought, 'Who knows? The Lord may be gracious to me and let the child live.' But now that he is dead, why should I go on fasting? Can I bring him back again? I will go to him, but he will not return to me.* (2 Samuel 12:20-21)

David accepted an unfathomable loss, this discipline from his heavenly Father. He went to the house of the Lord and worshiped. David felt the rod and blessed God. He was, by God's supernatural power, clothed in meekness.

You see meekness is both exposed, and grows, when we are provoked. Sometimes our provocations are in the form of *deserved* discipline, like David's was after adultery and murder. Other times they are in the form of undeserved criticism, like David's encounter with Shimei.

HE THAT IS DOWN FEARS NO FALL

Remember our working definition of meekness, *an attitude of humility toward God and gentleness toward people flowing from trust that God is loving and in control.* David fits that definition to a T. He was humble toward God and gentle toward a hateful man named Shimei.

Shimei was a pain in King David's neck. He was a distant relative of King Saul, and a bitter provocateur. Now, decades after Saul's death, he still resents David's kingship. Shimei is not afraid to kick a man—even a king—when he's down.

Here's the scene: King David is running for his life, fleeing a hostile takeover by his usurper son Absalom. He and his loyal followers are just outside the city when they hear Shimei's heckling: "Get out, get out, you worthless man.

The LORD has brought upon you all the blood of the house of Saul… you are caught in your own evil" (2 Samuel 16:8).

To which Abishai, a loyal, right-hand man asks, "Why should this dead dog curse my lord the king? Let me go over and cut off his head."

A less meek, wounded dog may have consented. But not David. He didn't let Abishai take revenge even though it was well within his power as King. Instead, a hint of something comes through in David's response. A realization, perhaps, that God is working something out through this cursing critic.

Can you hear notes of this in David's reply?

> *Behold, my own son seeks my life; how much more now may this Benjaminite! Leave him alone, and let him curse, for the Lord has told him to. It may be that the Lord will look on the wrong done to me, and that the Lord will repay me with good for his cursing today.* (2 Samuel 16:11b-12)

This is the long view. This is the humble road. This is strong and this is meek. God must be at work here!

Even though Shimei's walking path was up high, his ways were down low.

> *As David and his men went along the road, Shimei went along the hillside opposite him and cursed as he went, threw stones at him and kicked up dust.* (2 Samuel 16:11-13)

John Bunyan[4], the author of *The Pilgrim's Progress* said: "He that is down fears no fall." King David is down, running from his rebel son while Shimei goes alongside, hurling curses and stones. Abishai offers to defend the king and lop off Shimei's head.

But remember that the meek "look past second causes." They trust that behind all that happens to them, is a good Father who uses it for them. Author Alan Redpath[5] notes that:

> *David even received the cursing of his enemies as part of the discipline of God… All the curses and abuse that could ever come to him were simply the ministry of God to help him toward perfection and restoration.*

David kissed the rod. He says, "Let him be," doesn't defend himself, and like Joseph and Moses and the great Son of David, he leaves vengeance to God. David lets hateful Shimei speak.

WHY THE MEEK DEAL GENTLY

Bible teacher David Guzik[6] offers three reasons why David let Shimei curse. Guzik doesn't use the word *meek*, but by now, we hear it loud and clear.

David let Shimei speak because:

1. **He saw the hand of God in every circumstance.** "The LORD has told him to" (2 Samuel 16:11). He knew that God was able to shut Shimei up; David didn't need to give the order.

2. **He put the "Shimei problem" in perspective.** "See how my son who came from my own body seeks my life. How much more now may this Benjamite?" (2 Samuel 16:11). David knew that his root problem was his own son Absalom, not Shimei, and he did not lose this perspective.

3. **He knew that God's hand was on the future as well as the present.** "It may be that the LORD will look on my affliction, and that the LORD will repay me with good for his cursing this day" (2 Samuel 16:12). David knew that God would take care of his future.

Notice that knowing these things *didn't* stop David's grief. In 2 Samuel 15:30, we read:

> *David continued up the Mount of Olives, weeping as he went; his head was covered and he was barefoot. All the people with him covered their heads too and were weeping as they went up.*

Why did David weep? Author Paul Tripp[7] develops two lines of thought on this question:

> *This is a monarchy—in order for Absalom to take the throne, David must die. David weeps for the people he loves, people he can no longer lead.*

> *But there is another reason for David's weeping....When Nathan confronted David with the sin of adultery and murder, he predicted that evil would rise from the house of David against him—as a direct result of David's sin. He is not just mourning his son. He is mourning the consequences of his sin.*

The man after God's own heart had experienced God's forgiveness (Psalm 32:1). But he still mourned the consequences of his sin. His sin with Bathsheba brought life-long hardship on himself, his family and his kingdom. So David wept.

But as Paul tells us (2 Corinthians 7:10), "godly sorrow brings repentance that leads to salvation and leaves no regret." We do well to weep over our sin, as David did. And yet, we cannot miss the fact that he slept. Psalm 3:5 says, "I lie down and sleep; I wake again, because the Lord sustains me."

David wrote that. But do you know when?

The superscript over the third Psalm reads, "A psalm of David. When he fled from his son Absalom. David wrote those words when he had every reason *not* to sleep.

In a message on Psalm 3, entitled, "How to Get a Good Night's Sleep," Pastor Kevin DeYoung[8] explains,

> *"When David wrote "How many are my foes!" (Psalm 3:1), he is not just waxing poetic. There were literally thousands of people risen against him. David had massive, life-threatening, family-disintegrating, career-shattering problems."*

There was an army trying to kill him. His own son hated him to death. His family had turned against him. Yet God was a shield about him, his glory, and the lifter of his head. So David slept.

So, here's the pressing question: "Do you take discipline like David?" How do you take corrections and how do you handle consequences? In the face of discipline, David did what strong, meek, maturing children of God do. They don't despair, but they also don't blow it off.

> *My son, do not make light of the Lord's discipline of the Lord, and do not lose heart when he rebukes you.* (Hebrews 12:5b, NIV)

The meek avoid both extremes.

Like David. David didn't take God's discipline lightly. He didn't "blow it off" as if his sin was no big deal. He wept. But he also didn't crumble into a heap. David did what the meek do when they're disciplined: He confessed his sin and trusted God's love. Then he slept.

He wept then he slept. At the moment we kiss the rod of his discipline, meekness is being formed in us. We are growing into men and women after God's heart.

David's is a tough act to follow.

MELTING WHEN GOD LIFTS YOUR HEAD

Recently, a friend cared enough to confront me about some unkind words I had spoken to her. After listening, I wholeheartedly agreed. I was dead wrong.

But I hung my head. I was a puppy cowering beside her on the bench, my tail between my legs. I was losing heart. She gently, boldly called me on that too.

"Why are you sitting like that, with your head down?"

I'm a complex case and I know it. But a big part of the answer was the obvious one. I still don't like to be corrected. And I'm working my way out of some entrenched meek*less*-coping skills. Before meekness, I was afflicted with the "all of nothing" syndrome when faced with unwelcome corrections.

Do you know someone who copes with correction this way? It usually looks like this on me. When I realize I've hurt someone, I want to disengage and walk away. To avoid addressing it. To hide. Pretend. That's the "nothing" in this silly syndrome. Or, I do the opposite. I go hyper-verbal on my corrector, defending my cause and explaining why her thin skin is the problem. That's the "all." Neither produce good fruit.

That's not what we learn from David. All-or-nothing is not how the man after God's own heart took discipline. What about you? Do you take discipline like David? Do you become soft? Compliant? Do you melt?

Like Jesus, David "entrusted himself to him who judges justly" (1 Peter 2:23). He didn't face off with Shimei. He accepted that hard words were coming his way because he trusted God. When you face discipline, even from the mouth of a sinful man, do you let the LORD be your shield, your glory and the lifter of your head?

My friend Jen told me a story about her four-year-old. Grace did something very naughty one morning. She made a mural on the wall with Jen's Sharpies.

So they had a talk. Then Jen sent Grace to her room.

At lunchtime, Grace slunk back to the kitchen, chin down, eyes glued to the floor. Jen loves Grace. That's why she disciplined her in the first place, why she knelt beside her, why she stroked her tear-smeared cheeks and why she did what God does with us. She lifted up her child's head.

And then Grace did what meek children do. She melted in her mama's hug.

What about you? Are you moving toward David's wept-then-slept response? Do you humbly accept God's discipline while trusting in His love? Do you receive his mercy and grace?

David did. It is no surprise that David was able to rest in the midst of all this turmoil. The words immediately after the account of Shimei's nastiness are:

> *Now the king and all the people who were with him became weary; so they refreshed themselves there.* (2 Samuel 16:14)

David was able to receive refreshment and comfort from God because he was at peace. Oh, yes, "the meek will inherit the land and enjoy great peace" (Psalm 37:11). David knew that God was in control of his kingdom and of his very life, even though hardships were bound to come. The meek claim Puritan Jeremiah Burroughs'[9] words:

> *The Lord sees further than I do; I only see things at present but the Lord sees a great while from now. And how do I know but that had it not been for this affliction, I should have been undone.*

We can kick against His discipline and harden our proud hearts against it. We can resist and refuse to accept it. And then we will become callous and hard. Or we can become more meek. David chose the latter, and became a man after God's heart.

When we receive discipline without losing heart, but still taking it to heart, this is to kiss the rod—and this, too, is meek.

FOR FURTHER REFLECTION:

1. What is your natural response to being corrected or shown where you were wrong? On the scale of 1 to 5, with 1 being "very defensive" and 5 being "very meek," where would you be on that scale, and why did you select that number?

2. If meekness is "accepting God's dealings, without murmuring, without sulking, without rebellion or resistance and the patient endurance of his will," then how does the incident with Shimei demonstrate meekness? How would you have responded to Shimei's insults?

3. Read Psalm 3 aloud. It is "a Psalm of David, when he fled from Absalom his son." What evidence of David's strength and meekness do you see in it? How does knowing the situation in which David penned this Psalm add to its meaning?

4. Read Hebrews 12:5-11. How does Hebrews 12:5 describe the two "un-meek" extremes for facing God's fatherly discipline?

5. Which do you find yourself falling into more often, losing heart or blowing it off? How did David respond when the child he conceived with Bathsheba grew sick, then died?

6. Does receiving God's discipline with meekness mean that we won't feel bad or put our heads down and cry? Why? Refer to 2 Corinthians 7:10 and Psalm 3:3.

7. Think back on the story of little Grace, the home graffiti artist. How is it an expression of meekness to let the God who disciplines us be "the lifter of our head"?

PRAYER OF RESPONSE

Dear Heavenly Father, thank you that you care enough about me to discipline me. Help me trust your love when I feel your correcting hand. Help me remember that you discipline those you love and that when I am corrected it is because I am your beloved child. Remind me that it is for my good, that I may share in your holiness. Thank you that you are the lifter of my head. I want to melt in your arms. Help me rest in your rich, free forgiveness you give when I turn to you.

Amen.

8 - Job: Meekness When Bereaved & Confused

Job still had questions. And Job still was hurting. But he knew that God was still in charge and God was still worthy to be praised.

—*Kevin DeYoung*[1]

The Lord gave, and the Lord has taken away; blessed be the name of the Lord.

–*Job, in Job 1:21*

By the time my sister began to labor with her second child, the baby was already with Jesus. That was twelve years ago. Grief comes in waves and life is never the same. My nieces and nephew talk about their sister Hope who is in heaven. It still hurts.

But Danielle and Andy know. They know that "the LORD will swallow up death forever and wipe away tears from all faces" (Isaiah 25:8). They know that "what is mortal will be swallowed up by life" (2 Corinthians 5:4). And, in real life and real time, they know "the God of hope" who fills them with all joy and peace in believing (Romans 15:13).

WHEN WE DON'T KNOW WHY

But there's something big they don't know. They don't know why. God didn't consult them beforehand, and has not revealed a reason since. I don't know Vaneetha Risner[3] personally, but she, too, has endured heart-rending loss—without knowing why. Vaneetha found peace in an unexpected way.

While I thought that freedom would be found in answers, true freedom was actually found in surrender. I didn't need to figure it out. It didn't need to make sense to me. I didn't need to understand the details. I just needed to trust God— because he is infinitely wiser, more loving, and more purposeful than I am. God always has a reason. He's probably got many, because He alone knows all the facts.

John Piper[4] says, "God is always doing 10,000 things in your life, and you may be aware of three of them." Or none. The meek believe this. Psalm 37:11 says, "the meek will inherit the land and delight themselves in abundant peace." Trusting that God has good reasons, even when they are unseen, explains how the meek can enjoy this peace. Believing there are good reasons for thwarted plans and for unspeakable losses is meek.

> He sends the storms and exposes—yea, demolishes—my building materials. Nothing now remains but Christ, no good but Him, no possession but Him, no confidence but Him. I choose Him by default—and incredibly He accepts that. Thou meekest divine suitor of my soul, You take me back again.
>
> —Andrée Seu Peterson[2]

In the weeks and months after Hope's funeral, my sister and brother-in-law did wonder why. We all wondered. But no doctor or test could explain. When precious things like health, dreams, or children are taken away, our faith in God's goodness is tried. Choosing to believe that our heavenly Father knows best is strong and meek and it brings peace.

But often before we reach that peaceful place, suffering leads us to think that God must be against us. Our enemy. This reaction goes way back thousands of years. The Bible describes this very human response to suffering in a man named Job. I won't recount all of Job's losses, but the first two chapters in Job describe the loss of his health and wealth, and the death of his seven sons and three daughters.

Job started strong. But as his suffering continued, patient Job wasn't perfect. His soul grew hot and over the course of thirty chapters, he began to question God's love. "His fury burns against me; he counts me as an enemy" (Psalm 19:11, New Living Translation). Questions flooded in. *Why me, why this, why now, why God, why?*

Spoiler alert: God *never* answered those questions. But in Job 38-41, God did challenge Job with no less than 55 rapid-fire questions to help Job see His power in his creation and to give Job perspective, even, in love, to teach him his place. In the last chapter, Job repents:

> *I have uttered what I did not understand, things too wonderful for me,*
> *which I did not know.* (Job 42:3)

We often utter what we don't understand, confused. Meekness trusts in the goodness of God. But, "things too wonderful?"

A MEEK SOUL WEANED

Things too wonderful rings a bell for me because that same phrase is found in Psalm 131, one of the meek-making verses I have claimed.

> *I do not concern myself with things too great or wonderful for me. But*
> *I have stilled and quieted my soul like a weaned child with its mother.*

If Job could say this after his wealth, health and children were taken away, surely I can say it when something as small as a church ministry opportunity was taken from me, right?

Wrong. My soul was not calm when I learned. It was not, to quote Psalm 131:2, "like a weaned child with its mother." My soul was more like a squirmy, squawky, 10-month-old, rooting and restless in his mother's lap. I had no peace.

My mind dialed back through the lead up to this decision.

Q: *Why wasn't my opinion sought?*

A: Because I was taken off the team.

Q: *But why was I taken off the team?*

A: Because the leader doesn't know me well.

Q: *But why…*

I won't tell you how far back I dialed, but it was more than five cause-effect loops deep. So I did what I often do when I need help unraveling my knotted, twisty thoughts. I went for a walk.

It wasn't till the home stretch that I recited Psalm 131 out loud:

> *I do not concern myself with things too great or wonderful for me. But I*
> *have stilled and quieted my soul like a weaned child with its mother."*

But I didn't just recite it by rote memory, I listened. The message there for me. By the last line, the Lord had stopped me cold. *Hold up, Abigail. Listen to my Word that you quote. Be still. Quit squirming. It's not your concern. This issue is too wonderful for you. You don't see the whole picture. Trust my reasons. Let it be.* I had peace. God has his reasons.

In Part I, we saw how the meek look past second causes. In my case, that meant refusing to get stuck analyzing the human decision makers who took away my opportunity. I'd been walking with meekness far too long to dwell there. I was learning to coach myself: *Trust that God was behind their decision, Abigail. Let it be.*

As the meek accept God's dealings with them as good, their resistance wanes. They trust that even the insults and injuries others inflict are for God's glory, including our maturity (see James 1:2-4). In other words, the meek trust that even when precious things are taken away, it is for good. "We don't say I don't deserve this and we shouldn't say I do deserve this. We should say I need this," notes author Jerry Bridges[5]. "That is the spirit of meekness. It is to realize that we need whatever God is bringing into our lives."

But to live supernaturally like this we must know what Job's first three friends did not know: that suffering is not distributed in this world in proportion to the evil or good a person does. It's not a matter of deserving or not deserving. Job was right when he boldly spelled out the difficult-to-grasp nature of this truth: "the wicked are spared in the day of calamity" (Job 21:30) while "the just and blameless man is a laughingstock" (Job 12:4). Those who suffer most may be pleasing God most, and those who prosper most may be *pleasing* him *least*. Christ leads the way here. The holy Son of God, "was made perfect by what he suffered," (Hebrews 2:10). No servant is above his master. So it shouldn't surprise us that even when we do the right thing, even when we obey, even when we are lined up with God's will, we still face troubles (Matthew 5:10; John 16:33).

The meek say, "Yes, God is in control. He is just and wise. Even though suffering and success often seem to come randomly in this life, all wrongs will be righted in the life to come. He has shown me his love in Christ Jesus. I know he is the only hope for meaning in this life now and for salvation in the life to come. So I will trust God, though I don't understand his ways." Many Christians live at this level of understanding.

Yet God has revealed *some* of his ways. The meek press deeper with the writer of Job. He wants us to know that God has not hidden all of his reasons. Job's friend Elihu shows us more of God's purpose in suffering than we typically see.

GOD'S REVEALED REASONS

Job's first three friends, not including Elihu, assumed that his suffering was proof of his sinfulness and God's displeasure. If we're honest, we might even acknowledge that we behave as if we believe a strain of that ourselves. When we see people suffer, sometimes our first thought is that they somehow had it coming. On the flipside, we think that when we keep our noses clean, we'll be spared. As much as we hate to admit it, deep down, some of us might wonder if troubles are proof of the sufferer's wrongdoing.

That is how the first three friends, Eliphaz, Bildad, and Zophar made sense of Job's troubles. They had two categories for people: righteous and sinner. The righteous don't suffer. Sinners do. Cut and dry. They missed the biblical category of the "righteous sufferer."

For God to call a person righteous does not mean that the person is sinlessly perfect, rather they chose to seek God and turn from sin. Only one was sinless, and only through faith in Christ we are declared righteous (Romans 3:28, Philippians 3:9). Back to the point at hand: God repeatedly called Job a righteous man (Job 1:1, 1:8, 2:3) and still allowed so much to be taken from him. So we are faced with this third category: the righteous sufferer.

But why permit the righteous to suffer? That's where Elihu's message comes in. From him, we learn something that neither Job nor his friends knew, at least until he spoke. He offers another perspective on why the righteous suffer. We read it in Job 36:15:

> *He delivers the afflicted by their affliction and opens their ear by adversity.*

That is Elihu's theology for the suffering of the righteous. That God "delivers the afflicted *by* their affliction." How? By opening their ear and instructing them in the midst of their trials (Job 36:10). That sounds a lot like Psalm 119:71:

> *It was good for me that I was afflicted, that I might learn your statutes.*

Don't we discover more of God's sovereign goodness, more of his sufficient grace, more of his unsearchable wisdom, and Shepherd-care in our dark nights than in our bright days? God delivers the afflicted *by* their affliction. He shows us our need of him and meets it.

From Elihu we learn that the suffering of the righteous is not a sign of God's indignant anger but of his redeeming love. It is not "the punishment of their sins but a refinement of their righteousness. It is not a preparation for destruction, but a protection from destruction."[6] God uses our suffering to open our ears to him.

JOB'S WRONG ASSUMPTIONS (& OURS)

In his attempts to make sense of his own suffering, Job also made wrong assumptions.

His first was to assume that his trials were random. Who could blame him? After all, he was right when he observed that "the wicked are spared in the day of calamity" (Job 21:30), while "the just and blameless man is a laughingstock" (Job 12:4). Job was also sorely mistaken when he assumed that God was his enemy (Job 13:24, 19:11, 33:10). His suffering was not random nor was God his enemy.

Why such suffering for the righteous? "That he may turn man aside from his deed, and cut off pride from man, and keep back his soul from the pit" (Job 33:17). Here Elihu does *not* picture God as an angry judge, "but as a Redeemer, a Savior, a Rescuer, a Doctor."[7] Yes, a surgeon's knife wounds, but not like an enemy's sword. Suffering "opens the ears of men" (33:16a). "Pain is God's megaphone," C.S. Lewis[8] so poignantly says. Trials received this way can make us more sensitive to our remaining pride and help us to turn from it to our loving Lord, as we become more used to his steady, skillful hand.

God loves us as we are, one iteration goes, but too much to leave us that way. Sometimes he uses our troubles to help us learn his ways. It means we can receive hard circumstances as training, as discipline, as opportunities to grow in holiness (Hebrews 12:10)—which is to say to become more like Jesus. This is neither punishment nor a random act. It is kind and purposeful.

This meek mindset interprets our trials, not as a sign of God's displeasure, of as evidence of God's redeeming love. The meek begin to see that there are aspects of godliness that can *only* be learned through trials. By grace, they still and quiet their souls. They grow in their ability to rest in Christ, content.

Rest comes easier in suffering when we know that God is not our enemy. He loves us (1 John 3:1). He is for us (Romans 8:31). He calls us friends (John 15:15). This means that our concepts of "for us" and "loving us" must somehow also include "taking away." Loving and being "for" his children means that sometimes God removes. Bittersweet as it is, the meek trust that "though God wounds, he will also heal" (Job 5:18).

In his bereavement and confusion, Job attributed the root cause of his great loss to God. This is hard to grasp. Yet we hear this meek response from Job first when a servant escapes to tell him that all his children had died when a wind of God, struck his oldest son's house:

> *Then Job arose and tore his robe and shaved his head and fell on the ground and worshiped. And he said, "Naked I came from my mother's womb, and naked shall I return. The Lord gave, and the Lord has taken away; blessed be the name of the Lord."*
>
> *In all this Job did not sin or charge God with wrong.* (Job 1:20-22)

Then, as if to make sure we don't miss the point, we see almost the same words in Job 2. After Satan got God's permission to afflict provided he spared Job's life, we read:

> *Satan went out from the presence of the Lord and struck Job with loathsome sores from the sole of his foot to the crown of his head. And he took a piece of broken pottery with which to scrape himself while he sat in the ashes.*
>
> *Then his wife said to him, "Do you still hold fast your integrity? Curse God and die."*

Now be ready to be amazed at how Job answers her (Job 2:10):

> *You speak as one of the foolish women would speak. Shall we receive good from God, and shall we not receive evil?*

Get ready. Because Scripture's Author wants us to know that Job was not misspeaking, that he was absolutely right.

> *In all this Job did not sin with his lips.*

Job didn't turn back from that line. He looked past the secondary cause of his grief, past the devil on leash to the God who held the leash, and in the most poignant of phrases, affirmed his faith yet again:

> *Though he slay me, I will hope in him.* (Job 13:15a)

Don't miss the focal point of the case I'm making. Our good Father not only gives but *also* takes away, and when he does it is always for his children's good. Believing that allows us to hope right on and praise him still. Worshiping our way *through* grief is at the very heart of meekness.

There is one more verse that brings us deeper still into this challenging truth. It's in the last chapter of Job, right after God gave him "twice as much as he had before." I admit, it blew my mind when I first took note of the phrase. Are you ready for this?

> *Then came to him all his brothers and sisters and all who had known him before, and ate bread with him in his house. And they showed him sympathy and comforted him for all the evil that the Lord had brought upon him. And each of them gave him a piece of money and a ring of gold.* (Job 42:11)

All of the evil that the Lord had brought upon him. Not "all the evil that Satan," or even wild nature, "had brought on him." The Lord Almighty is telling us that everything that happened to Job came, even if indirectly, from God who knows what we don't, sees what we can't and understands what we won't fully understand until we stand face to face. "Even if He causes grief, He will show compassion according to His steadfast love" (Lamentations 3:32).

Job was *not* mistaken when he said, "The Lord gives and the Lord takes away."

THE COMPASSIONATE, MERCIFUL PURPOSE OF THE LORD IN OUR SUFFERING

Neither was James wrong when he wrote, "Behold, we consider those blessed who remained steadfast. You have heard of the steadfastness of Job, and you have seen the purpose of the Lord, how the Lord is compassionate and merciful" (James 5:11). Scripture affirms God's compassion and mercy over and over.

But where exactly do we find it in Job?

It is there. But I admit, I needed help seeing it. My *ESV Study Bible*[9] came to my aid with these notes on chapter 38, verse 1 when God "spoke to Job out of the whirlwind."

> *God reveals himself to Job in a display of both majestic power and relational presence: "the LORD" (Hebrew YHWH), the name most used to signify God's covenant character and promises, was used in the prologue where God describes Job's relationship to him (see Job 1:8; 2:3); the fact that the Lord "answered Job" contrasts with what the friends...indicated he should expect (see 35:9-13)...It is a covenantal gesture when the Lord reveals his power and his presence as he speaks to Job "out of the whirlwind." While he does not come simply to justify Job, the Lord's presence shows that his reproof comes in the context of steadfast love toward Job and not as judgment for what the friends*

assumed was Job's repudiation of the path of righteousness.

Do you see it? The compassion and mercy of the Lord is in his revealing himself to Job, and not in judgment. God shows his love by sharing his presence. A living relationship with our covenant God is the best, longest-lasting, stability-making gift that we could ever receive. The fact that God came to Job personally indicates his care. The use of his covenantal name shows he is speaking to Job in the context of an active, committed, loving relationship.

This is how God shows Job, and us, his compassion and mercy. In his presence. Part of that mercy, of his gracious purpose, is to affirm that he is more precious than possessions, family, or health. It is to refine our faith and to prove that he is the strength of our hearts and our portion forever. He may take away to focus our hope, so that, as the Psalmist wrote, our souls find rest in God alone (Psalm 62:1). The Lord is compassionate and merciful. Sometimes He even takes away to draw us closer still to his glory.

In the last lines of M. S. Nicholson's poem,"The Thorn,"[10] we see this purpose of God piercingly described,

> *I took it home and though at first the cruel thorn hurt sore,*
> *As long years passed I learned at last to love it more and more.*
> *I learned He never gives a thorn without this added grace,*
> *He takes the thorn to pin aside the veil which hides His face.*

"The Lord gives and the Lord has taken away. Blessed be the name of the Lord," (Job 1:21) are meek words. The Lord took away beloved children, and David and Job and my sister and brother-in-law found their way to worship. Worship found them. Meekness found them. This is what the Puritan writers meant when they said "He kissed the rod and blessed God." Our sacrifice of praise displays the great worth of Christ in our hearts.

This is one of God's *revealed* purposes in taking away.

Job wasn't perfect, though. God had to correct him. You can read exactly how He did that in Job 38-41. But Job *did not sin* when he received both good and evil, both the gift and the taking away of the gift, as ultimately from God's hand.

Kevin DeYoung[11] says simply, "Job loved God when he had everything, and he loved God when he had nothing. Job still had questions. And Job still was hurting. But he knew that God was still in charge and God was still worthy to be praised."

When we trust God with our unanswered whys, when we place our hope in his good purposes, and bless his name when he takes away, this is meek. DeYoung[12] concludes:

> *God will turn around our suffering just like he did for Job. But he may not do it right away. Some of God's people suffer through many trials all through life. Even so, God promises to bless those who stay close to him. For some the blessing comes soon. For others it comes in heaven. But for all of God's children, the best blessing is God himself.*

Sometimes God graciously shares what he is up to and why. But many other times, for wise reasons He alone knows, He does not fully disclose. Job did not get all the answers, but he got God's presence and a greater experience of His care. With those, Job was satisfied.

When with Job, may we say, "The Lord gave, and the Lord has taken away; blessed be the name of the Lord"—this, too, is meek.

FOR FURTHER REFLECTION:

1. When something you value is taken away—whether a dream, an object, or even a person—how do you respond?

2. Thinking back, how has your reaction to something or someone you loved being taken away changed?

3. The divine Author of Job wanted it to be crystal clear about the ultimate source of Job's losses. Review Job 1:20-22, Job 2:10, Job 13:15 and Job 42:11. Who was ultimately behind Job's losses?

4. In James 5:11 we read, "You have heard of the steadfastness of Job, and you have seen the purpose of the Lord, how the Lord is compassionate and merciful." Where do you see God's compassion and mercy to Job? Do you struggle with this?

5. One of the lessons we learn from Job is that suffering is not random. It is, John Piper says, "apportioned to us as individually designed, expert therapy by the loving hand of our great Physician. And its aim is that our faith might be refined, our holiness might be enlarged, our soul might be saved, and our God might be glorified." Where do you see the loving purposes described in these texts to be true in your life?

   • 1 Peter 1:6–7

   • Hebrews 12:10–11

   • 2 Corinthians 1:8–9

   • James 1:2–4

6. The other purpose of God in our suffering, that we can know this side of heaven, is to prove that he is more precious than anything else. Can you think of a loss that helped you see God himself as more precious?

7. M. S. Nicholson wrote, "I learned He never gives a thorn without this added grace, He takes the thorn to pin aside the veil which hides His face." How might this thorn image help you worship God in what feels like a forsaken, lonely place?

PRAYER OF RESPONSE

Dear Lord, help me to bless your name when I feel the pain of what you've taken away. Help me to count it all joy when I meet trials of various kinds, because you promise that the testing of my faith is productive and will produce endurance so that I may be perfect and complete, lacking in nothing.

Amen.

9 - Paul: Meekness When Disappointed & Alone

Do you sulk or do you have the meekness that can be wounded by the sharp arrow of hatred but not get embittered or resentful?

—*Elisabeth Elliot'*

At my first defense no one came to stand by me, but all deserted me. May it not be charged against them! But the Lord stood by me and strengthened me, so that through me the message might be fully proclaimed...

—*Paul, 2 Timothy 4:16-17a*

You would think a 47-year-old mother wouldn't still be grieving the children she never had. But grief and disappointment come at their own pace, uncontrolled, in waves. And sometimes this mom still does.

One wave hit me when a friend posted a photo of four adorable kids walking along a sunbathed farm path, two blue-jeaned kids walking hand in hand, and a third pulling a red wagon full of the toddler fourth. The caption read, "I love watching them become best friends." Another wave washed over me as I sat with my friends and their five children, flipping cards and grabbing spoons at the dining room table. In the moment, I kept my smile. But in bed that night, I cried myself dry.

WHEN DREAMS DIE

Maybe your disappointment is a dream smashed by an injury, a breakup or some great loss. Maybe your hope for reconciliation or healing, for marriage or children, or for satisfying, paying work has slowly fizzled out. Maybe your father and mother have forsaken you (Psalm 27:10) and your friends have left you in a lurch. Or maybe the waves radiate from a smaller quake.

Like spring break plans falling through. The details don't matter so much, except to say that it didn't work out as we planned. When we canceled our Sanibel reservation last spring so my husband could take a trip, we were given dibs on time off for the following year's spring break travel. So we booked the condo and we made our plans. But when the time came, his time-off request was denied. Turns out the "dibs" weren't enough to secure our space.

I was irate. That meant Jim could not have the week. He had to work. Since the boys and I only had that week off, it meant we couldn't take spring break. But Jim is a man of peace, and more meek than me. I would have pressed harder. But Jim valued peace. Although he felt disappointed, he soon accepted this kink in our plans, this "crook in the lot." He was used to God's hand, even when it came through "dibs" that didn't stick.

Eventually, I came around. But it took a few months. I was starting to learn that inordinate grief or misplaced anger might reveal an idol. Remember, the meek one is a lion for *God's* cause, a lamb for its own. My angry grief was a warning light on the dashboard of my heart. I wanted Sanibel more than I wanted God's will. Emotions are great revealers. They are lights on the dashboard, and what I do with them determines how the car drives. How I cope with disappointment reflects on my understanding of God. The Spirit reminded me that if I am discontent with my situation, it means that I have more to learn about my Father's provision. When we lean into providence and trust God's goodness in the face of disappointment, that puts God's greatness on display.

It also steers me toward meekness when I think of self-pity and entitlement crouching at disappointment's door. They tempt me to resist God's fatherly hand the second my plans fall through. They like to remind me how badly I was wronged and how I deserve so much better. Those meekness rivals would have me resist God's taming grace. They drive out contentment and they do not deliver life.

Strengthened by grace, we fight back. We take up "the sword of the Spirit which is the word of God" (Ephesians 6:17). It's probably low on most lists of fighter verses but Ecclesiastes 7:14 inflicts a blow. "Consider the work of God, for who can make straight what God has made crooked?"

That truth is a taming grace when it seems my trials are out of God's control.

DISAPPOINTMENT—HIS APPOINTMENT

Thomas Boston[3] wrote an entire book on that one verse. It called *"The Crook in the Lot."* I know it's an odd title. *Crook* is short for *crooked*, and *lot* means *situation*, as in one's "lot in life." The alternate title, *The Sovereignty and Wisdom of God Displayed in the Afflictions of Men*, tells all.

The book was published in 1737, but Boston's words are timeless. Because as long as life endures, there will be trials. But we see the pain redeemed, and allow ourselves to be shaped by God's hand and tamed—rather than embittered—by disappointment, when we think with kingdom minds.

> *I would rather be afflicted, feeling that it is "the appointment of God," than feeling that it is "by chance" or "haphazard." It speaks comfort to the afflicted children of God to consider that whatever the crook in your lot is, it is of God's making and therefore you may look upon it kindly since it is your Father who made it for you. Question not but that there is a favorable design in it toward you."*

But trusting God's "favorable design" when our plans fall apart doesn't mean the meek won't experience disappointment. Rather, the meek have trained themselves to look past the second cause to the loving, taming hand of God. It doesn't mean they are never wounded by hurtful or hateful people. We can be wounded.

But will we allow ourselves to get trapped by entitlement and self-pity?

Author Elisabeth Elliot[4] asked, "Do you sulk or do you have the meekness that can be wounded by the sharp arrow of hatred but not get embittered or resentful?" Jesus, the King of Meekness was wounded, mortally wounded. Isaiah's prophecy of the "Suffering Servant" leaves no question of that. "But he was pierced for our transgressions; he was crushed for our iniquities; upon him was the chastisement that brought us peace, and with his wounds we are healed" (Isaiah 53:5). But it also leaves no doubt about his meekness. "He was oppressed, and he was afflicted, yet he opened not his mouth; like a lamb that is led to the slaughter, and like a sheep that before its shearers is silent, so he opened not his mouth" (Isaiah 53:7).

When we receive our "crooked lots" and take our wounds without resentment, when we love and trust on through our deep disappointment, we are more like Jesus. This, I think, is at least part of how God "beautifies the meek" (Psalm 149:4, King James Bible).

Even as they grieve the path they thought they would take, the meek know that God is guiding. They cling to the promise that the meek will inherit the land.

In other words, meekness knows that our disappointment is God's appointment. That his grace comes often in the wilderness, and that when God makes our way crooked, for the time being, it must be better than straight. Oh, yes, Proverbs 3:6 is true: the Lord makes our path straight as we lean into him (Proverbs 3:6). But he might make it crooked first.

It just so happens that the day after I cried myself dry, I discovered this quaint old poem.

> *"Disappointment — His Appointment"*
> *Change one letter, then I see*
> *That the thwarting of my purpose*
> *Is God's better choice for me.*
> *His appointment must be blessing,*
> *Tho' it may come in disguise,*
> *For the end from the beginning*
> *Open to His wisdom lies.*
>
> *"Disappointment — His Appointment"*
> *Whose? The Lord, who loves me best,*
> *Understands and knows me fully,*
> *Who my faith and love would test;*
> *For, like a loving earthly parent,*
> *He rejoices when He knows*
> *That His child accepts...,*
> *All that from His wisdom flows.*
>
> *"Disappointment — His Appointment"*
> *"No good thing will He withhold,"*
> *From denials oft we gather*
> *Treasures of His love untold,*
> *Well He knows each broken purpose*
> *Leads to fuller, deeper trust,*
> *And the end of all His dealings*
> *Proves our God is wise and just.*

"Disappointment — His Appointment"
Lord, I take it, then, as such.
Like the clay in hands of potter,
Yielding wholly to Thy touch.
All my life's plan in Thy molding,
Not one single choice be mine;
Let me answer, unrepining —
"Father, not my will, but Thine."

—Laura Sophia Soole[5]

But we dare not sugarcoat. We dare not make this neat. Meekness is not natural or easy. It is a fruit of God's Spirit. To receive disappointment and broken plans as God's wise appointment is a gift given to those who clothe themselves with meekness (Colossians 3:12). This way through trials is supernatural. Of course, we find ourselves asking God, "What are you doing to me?" Meekly, we come to understand that God never allows anything to be done *to* us that isn't also *for* us.

The Apostle Paul knew this. He was a meek master. Over and over, we see Paul's "brokenhearted boldness." We see him "admonishing every one" boldly but "with tears, "brokenhearted tears (Acts 20:31). When Paul had to share hard words and corrections, he sought to imitate "the meekness and gentleness of Christ" (2 Corinthians 10:1). When he told the Galatian believers how to help those caught in sin, he said to do it in a spirit of *prautes* or meekness (Galatians 6:1). We can also look at his thorn in the flesh and how he meekly received it: "For the sake of Christ, then, I am content with weaknesses, insults, hardships, persecutions, and calamities. For when I am weak, then I am strong" (2 Corinthians 12:10). From the blinding light on the Damascus road, Paul's story was that of a strong man, tamed by God's grace. In his affliction and abuse, in correction and insults, Paul was meek.

But it's the last chapter of his last New Testament letter that we'll study now. Paul is in a prison in Rome. He knows his time is short. Paul is on trial for his life. In fact, scholars suggest he may have died within weeks of writing his last letter to Timothy.

The time of my departure has come. I have fought the good fight, I have finished the race, I have kept the faith. Henceforth is laid up for me a crown of righteousness. (2 Timothy 4:7-9a)

Surprisingly, Paul does not close on this hopeful, triumphant note. Instead, he returns to his present predicament imprisoned in Rome. I love how theologian John Stott[6] describes the situation:

> *Apostle Paul, great and godly man as he was, was a man of flesh and blood. He was a man of like passions with us and although he has finished his course and although he is awaiting his crown, he is still a frail human being with ordinary human needs.*

Paul, mighty as he was, suffered loneliness. His friends had deserted him. He was separated from the churches he founded and the church friends he knew and loved. Demas deserted him. Crescens went to Galatia, Titus to Dalmatia, and Tychicus to Ephesus. "Luke alone is with me" (2 Timothy 4:10-12a). For various reasons, good and bad, Paul is in Rome, in prison, alone.

> Don't get so super-spiritual that you say you're above the need of human friendships. If you're as super-spiritual as that, you are super-scriptural."
>
> —John Stott

How does Paul react? How does a mighty meek man manage such severe disappointment? He begs Timothy, "Do your best to come soon" (2 Timothy 4:9)—while I'm still alive, before winter, when you can still cross the sea. Paul wanted his friends. He had set his hope on the coming of Christ but his longing for friendship continued to burn strong. Theologian John Stott asserts,

> *(Human friendship) is the provision of God for men. Wonderful as is the presence of Jesus with us today, wonderful is the prospect of his coming, there are no substitutes for human friends. Paul wanted Timothy.*

The place of his captivity must have been cold. So Paul also wanted a cloak to keep his body warm and books and parchments to keep his mind occupied (2 Timothy 4:13).

The meek can be wounded. While they may handle hardship with supernatural grace, they still experience disappointment, loneliness, and grief. I include this section because I want you to know that this side of heaven, even the strongest, most mature of saints of great faith, can be hurt. Paul's words in 2 Timothy 4 show us that although the Lord is always with us, we should not despise the use of means. In other words, God's grace may come directly from him to us

– seemingly out of thin air as it were–but more often than not, it comes through tangible means. To quote Stott[7] again,

> *When our spirit is lonely, we need friends. When our body is cold, we need clothing, When our mind is bored, we need books. These things are not unspiritual, they are human. It is the need of an ordinary frail and mortal man. Don't get so super-spiritual that you say you're above the need of human friendships. If you're as super-spiritual as that, you are super-scriptural.*

Trusting God's love and care in our disappointment is meek. Asking for what we need is meek. Receiving what the Lord provides is meek. To be clear, meekness does not preclude the use of God's kind means. He provides people and things to satisfy our needs. God works through physicians, therapists, counselors and teachers. He works through medicine, exercise and sunshine. To request books, cloaks, and friends, to seek wise counsel and caring community is not weak. It is humbly accepting that our Good Father uses these means to reach our deep needs.

PAUL'S TRIUMPHANT GETHSEMANE

Paul's meekness is expressed in two magnificent ways in the last letter he ever wrote. We find him cold, lonely, and longing for his books. Alexander the coppersmith, he notes, has done him "great harm," and he warns Timothy to "be on guard" (2 Timothy 4:14-15). He laments the fact that "no one came to stand by me, but all deserted me" (2 Timothy 4:16). At his first trial, not a single soul came to give sympathy or support. "This moment was Paul's Gethsemane," Stott says[8], "for like his Master, he was alone in his great ordeal. And in his greatest need all his friends forsook him and fled."

How Paul responds now is a breathtaking display of meekness. Will Paul break down? Will we find some trace of self-pity or pride? Some evidence that those meekness counterfeits snared him? Will we find Paul sulking, wallowing in self-pity? Certainly now that he is in grave personal danger his consuming concern will turn to himself, right?

Wrong. It does not. It is Christ. Paul's main concern is not to plead his own cause but the cause of Jesus Christ. We see that in 2 Timothy 4:17 in the words, "so that."

> *The Lord stood with me and strengthened me so that through me the message might be fully proclaimed and all the Gentiles might hear it.*

We rightly focus on the wonder that the Lord himself stood with Paul and strengthened him.

But why? Paul is crystal clear: "so that through me the message might be fully proclaimed." So in one of the highest courts in the whole Roman Empire, Paul preached Christ. We see the same meek mindset in Paul's letter to the Philippian church, "what has happened to me has really served to advance the gospel, so that it has become known throughout the whole imperial guard and to all the rest that my imprisonment is for Christ" (Philippians 1:12-13).

Let's not miss the second meek layer we see in Paul's last words. Recall that the meek commit their cause to God and trust him to ultimately avenge wrongs done to them. Like Jesus cleansing his Father's temple, a meek soul is a lion in God's cause, but a lamb in its own. The meek are able to forgive.

Immediately after he describes how his friends deserted him, Paul utters these amazing words, "May it not be charged against them!" He must have heard those words decades ago when he guarded the coats of Stephen's killers, "Do not hold this sin against them" (Acts 7:60). Those words sound a lot like his Lord's as he hung on the cross, "Father, forgive them, for they know not what they do" (Luke 23:34).

So we see the disappointments that would have been cause for despair and resentment for those less meek, as a cause for rejoicing in Paul (Colossians 1:24a). How was that possible? Because Paul chose to receive them as God's appointment. He chose to see them not as randomly landing, but as wisely assigned. Paul chose to accept the crook in his lot, and to use his prison as a platform to advance the gospel and preach Christ.

Our disappointments, crooked lots and kinked plans may pale by comparison to Paul's. The divine upside might not be so obvious in our less extreme circumstances. Paul watched as the imperial guard converted to Christianity because of this faithful, meek life he lived while imprisoned.

I still don't know exactly why our spring break trip got canceled. But I do know this. Whenever we can forgive those who let us down and trust God's wisdom when our plans go sideways, we become witnesses to our good God.

When, with Paul, we accept disappointment as God's loving appointment—this, too, is meek.

FOR FURTHER REFLECTION:

1. What disappointments have you faced lately? How did you respond to them?

2. Reread Philippians 1:12-18 and 1 Timothy 4:6-18. Paul wrote both letters from prison. Where did he see God's appointment in his circumstances?

3. Even though Paul responded with meekness to his disappointment and the desertion by friends, he still sought relief. As John Stott said, "this great man was still human." What three things did Paul ask for in 2 Timothy 4:9-13? How is this instructive for you?

4. Paul had no one with him when he stood trial in Rome. What was his response to standing trial alone?

5. How was his response in 2 Timothy 4:16 like Jesus' response on the cross, and like Stephen's response as he was stoned?

6. What Scripture truths can empower us to forgive those who disappoint us or let us down? These verses may help:

- Ephesians 4:32

- Colossians 3:13

- Matthew 6:14

7. When we trace the "history of grace" in our lives, we will probably find a "crooked lot," not a straight line. When the Israelites left Egypt, God led them in nearly the opposite direction of Canaan. Pastor Timothy Keller has said, "So often the history of grace in our lives follows this same path. God seems to be taking us away from where we thought we were going, but he's still leading us to the Promised Land." What disappointment can you ask God to use to lead to your "Promised Land," and to him?

PRAYER OF RESPONSE

Dear Righteous Judge, please help me to release the bitterness I feel toward those who have disappointed me. Help me to fight the good fight of faith, and keep my eyes on you as I run my race, so that I can joyfully await "the crown of righteousness, which the Lord, the righteous judge, will award to me and to all who have loved his appearing."

Amen.

DIGGING DEEPER II

Jesus: Meekness When Insulted & Misunderstood

Indeed what is commonly called "sensitiveness" is the most powerful engine of domestic tyranny. How we should deal with it in others I am not sure; but we should be merciless to its first appearance in ourselves.

—C.S. Lewis[1]

Good sense makes one slow to anger, and it is his glory to overlook an offense.

—Proverbs 19:11

Some kids aren't fazed by an entire hour in the timeout chair. Others cry at a look. My mom says I was the second type. Are you the sensitive type? Whether you are or you're not, is being sensitive a good, meek thing? If by sensitive you imagine thoughtful, sympathetic and tender-hearted, well then it is indeed a good and godly way to be.

But there's that other side of sensitivity too. Let's call it that sensitive. Jesus, the King of Meekness, wasn't that sensitive, so neither should we be. Because meekness is not that sensitive. This chapter is about the fragile, easily offended sensitive. The touchy, irritable sensitive. The quick-to-feel-injured-and-wounded sort of sensitivity. The so-thin-skinned-that-others-tiptoe-around-you-for-fear-of-hurting-your-feelings sensitive.

That sensitive.

Suppose you are on the thin-skinned, that sensitive side. Why does it matter?

It matters because this self-focused sensitivity quickly morphs into sulking and self-pity. Here's where we sensitive types need to be so careful. Because we might walk away and tell ourselves that we "just need some space"—and we might. But the silence of meekness is vastly different from the silence of sulking. One is a means of trusting God, while the other is a sort of weapon against the person who hurt us. As Oswald Chambers[3] quotably noted,

> *Self-pity is of the devil, and if I wallow in it I cannot be used by God for His purpose in the world.*

The meek must have soft hearts and thick skins.

This is part of the beautiful contrast that makes the meek so useful to God. The meek are easily steered by him, sensitive to his voice. But we are not sidelined by the insults and mistreatment from others. At least not if we follow in the footsteps of Jesus. Because our Lord was not.

JESUS WAS NOT *THAT* SENSITIVE

When Jesus reached the ruler's house and found his daughter dead, he said to the mourners, "Go away, for the girl is not dead but sleeping." The townspeople "laughed at him,"—the Lord of the universe. But Jesus didn't rebuff them or sulk. Instead, "when the crowd had been put outside, he went in and took her by the hand, and the girl arose" (Matthew 9:24-25). Jesus kept on, intent on doing the Father's will, gentle and set like flint.

Shortly after that Jesus cast out a demon. "And the crowds marveled, saying, 'Never was anything like this seen in Israel.' But the Pharisees said, 'He casts out demons by the prince of demons,'" (Matthew 9:33b-34). Again, Jesus kept quietly on, doing good. He didn't lash out or wilt. He was not that sensitive.

We might excuse clueless townspeople and jealous Pharisees for their mockery. But what about Christ's cousin, John the Baptist? Even dear John had his

> To know that there is no provocation given us at any time, but if it be graciously improved, there is good to be gotten by it. This is a holy and happy way of opposing our adversaries, and resisting evil.
>
> —*Matthew Henry*[2]

doubts. "Now when John heard in prison about the deeds of the Christ, he sent word by his disciples and said to him, "Are you the one who is to come, or shall we look for another?" (Matthew 11:2-3). Jesus used Isaiah's "blind will see, deaf will hear" prophecy to affirm that he was in fact the one. He dealt gently with John.

We can understand John's doubts. After all, he was in prison for preaching the truth of Christ's kingdom. But what about the people in his own hometown? Surely they would appreciate his "wisdom and his mighty works," right? Wrong. "Is not this the carpenter's son? Is not his mother called Mary? ... And they took offense at him" (Matthew 13:55, 57a). But Jesus didn't take offense at them. Nor did he mince words when he spoke the "prophet is not without honor" proverb back to them. Quietly he kept on—doing his Father's will.

His cousin John, his hometown's people, and even Christ's closest friends misunderstood his mission. When Jesus "began to show his disciples that he must go to Jerusalem and suffer many things, Peter took him aside and scolded him, saying, 'Far be it from you, Lord! This shall never happen to you,'" (Matthew 13:21b-23). Even though it must have pained him to be so utterly misunderstood by Peter—whom Christ nicknamed "Rock"—Jesus was simply not that sensitive. So Jesus answered Peter, "Get behind me, Satan! You are a hindrance to me. For you are not setting your mind on the things of God, but on the things of man" (Matthew 16:23).

Sometimes Jesus used words to set the record straight. Other times, his silence spoke volumes. But sometimes, all it took was a look.

The last snapshot of our not that sensitive and perfectly compassionate Lord Jesus (see, for example, Matthew 9:36, 14:14, 20:34) also features Peter. Jesus has just been arrested. In the courtyard, Peter is warming himself by the fire while watching the drama unfold. He'd already denied Jesus twice. As the third denial is rolling off his lips, the rooster crows.

> *And the Lord turned and looked at Peter. And Peter remembered the saying of the Lord, how he had said to him, "Before the rooster crows today, you will deny me three times. And he went out and wept bitterly."*
> *(Luke 22:61-62)*

Jesus *looked* at Peter. Just a look. Was it the tenderness in his body language, this silent meekness in Jesus that broke Peter's heart?

The softness of meekness breaks down hardness, even rock hardness. Maybe this is why missionary author Elisabeth Elliot[4] declared meekness, "the greatest supernatural power in the world." It rates up there with the greatest of these, with love. Meekness is not natural. Natural is to sulk or lash out when we are hurt, misunderstood, or worse. Supernatural is to return good when evil comes.

This is also called love.

THE NOT THAT SENSITIVE SORT OF LOVE

Love "is not irritable or resentful" (1 Corinthians 13:5b). It is not easily provoked. Even when:

- An outdated note spills out of a backpack, spelling out when kids should have a coat (mine didn't) and what a healthy home-packed lunch includes (mine didn't).
- A friend forgets you're gluten-free and bakes a batch of her famous chocolate chunk cookies for your birthday.
- A lady with double the legal limit of groceries forces her way into the express check out line just as you approach.
- Your friend, in passing, mentions that her hair once looked like yours— "you know, sort of that mousy brown color."
- A dinner companion sits around your table offering this observation about your cooking: "This blueberry pie tastes really good, even with the tough crust."

Are you touchy and fragile when things like that happen and comments like that come? Do they make you sulky and irritable? Do hurt feelings linger hours and days after the offense?

God's meek children are tender-hearted toward others and thick-skinned when it comes to hurts against them. Because the love of God, agape love, is neither touchy-feely nor touchy. God's children love and their love is not irritable or resentful.

Being *that sensitive* and meekness do not mix. Being *that* sensitive gives the enemy a toe in the door of your camp. It leaves an opening for all kinds of problems. Paul makes it plain that we must be vigilant against unforgiveness that comes with ongoing anger. "Be angry and do not sin; do not let the sun go down on your anger, and give no opportunity to the devil" (Ephesians 4:26-27). Forgiveness shuts the door on all that nonsense. Forgiveness is the great "stand against the schemes of the devil" (Ephesians 6:11b).

If we are inclined to believe that being *that sensitive* isn't akin to anger, we should pause and reflect. Think of the people you avoid or have avoided in the past. Did many of them hurt, offend or reject you first? Licking our wounds endlessly and indulging our anger are close cousins. And they are definitely *not* related to meekness.

"It is just as much a Christian duty," theologian John Blanchard[5] has said, "to avoid taking offense as it is giving offense." As we grow in meekness we aim to neither give nor take offense. We glean our cues from Jesus: "When he was reviled he did not revile in return" (1 Peter 2:23). If our perfect Lord did not lash out, how much power does meekness have over our relentless temptation to "revile in return?"

Meekness flows from the confidence that God is in control, and therefore, we don't have to be. We become more meek as we gain confidence that the Lord is *always* at work in this world, fulfilling his good purposes; that he will get the last word; that he will right all wrongs. That's what makes us meek. It's our trust in the Lord in trying times and with trying people.

Remember, meekness is our strength under God's control. In Part III we'll take a closer look at how we grow more meek. But for this chapter, we will consider how the belt of truth pairs with the garment of meekness.

Stand firm, then, having put on the belt of truth. (Ephesians 6:14a)

How does the belt of truth help us stand strong? When our core, our middle, the place where the belt of truth should be is ungirded, we are injury prone. We are sensitive. That sensitive. I love how author Priscilla Shirer[6] explains this connection.

> *When the core is weak, any strenuous activity will cause your backbone to move around more loosely, more unprotected, making the body increasingly susceptible to injury. Being injury prone is not only hard on joints and muscles; it's also hard on hearts and relationships. Sensitive to taking offense is one of the key ways Satan traps believers in his web of deception.*

That was new to me. Sensitivity is one of the key ways Satan traps believers in his web of lies.

Shirer[7] concludes: "When we are easily wounded and hurt by the words and actions of other people, and then choose to nurse those wounds instead of offering forgiveness and grace or overlooking, we provide the enemy opportunity."

Nursing wounds is not meek. Being easily offended is not strong. Forgiveness, grace and overlooking are. To grow in meekness, we must notice when we are easily wounded and when our endless licking of our wounds prevents them from healing. We must not let the words and actions, the provocations that pierce us, fester. They must let them roll off their backs into God's capable hands. This is what meekness is. It is resilient and reasonable. It rises above the offense. It is not quick to put on offense.

"Let your reasonableness be known to all" Paul wrote (Philippians 4:5). My Bible footnote[8] to this verse states that the Greek for "reasonableness" implies "a generous spirit that rises above offenses; a forbearing spirit."

Do people tiptoe around you? Or are you known for your reason-able-rise-above meekness?

3 MEMORABLE TRUTHS FOR THE THICK-SKINNED, SOFT-HEARTED MEEK

These three truths have helped me thicken my own thin skin as I seek to keep a soft and generous heart.

1. Do unto others by assuming the best.

> *"So whatever you wish that others would do to you, do also to them, for this is the Law and the Prophets"* (Matthew 7:12).

The first skin-thickening truth comes from the school of hard knocks. When we pause to reflect deeply, we realize that many, if not most, of the people who hurt us don't intend to. They don't mean harm. They don't mean anything really. We intuitively understand this because, when someone tells us we've hurt them, we inevitably say, "that was *totally unintended.*" They felt it as a personal affront, but we didn't aim at them. We weren't aiming at all.

We want those we've accidentally wounded to believe the best in us. So, shouldn't we believe the best in them?

C.S. Lewis[9] nailed this in his *Letters to an American Lady.*

> *I think what one has to remember when people "hurt" each other is that in 99 cases out of 100 they intended to hurt very much less, or not at all, and are often quite unconscious of the whole thing. I've learned this from the cases in which I was the "hurter." When I have been really wicked and angry and meant to be nasty, the other party never cared or even didn't notice. On the other hand, when I have found out*

afterwards that I had deeply hurt someone, it has nearly always been quite unconscious on my part.

James said, "We all stumble in many ways" (James 3:2a). Isn't it a precious gift when we stumble to have the ones we've unconsciously hurt, graciously believe the best in us?

2. It is glorious to overlook an offense.

"Good sense makes one slow to anger and it is to his glory to overlook an offense" (Proverbs 19:11).

In the original Hebrew language, the word "glory" conveys "beauty, honor, splendor" and even "adornment." It is meekness. This is what Paul calls us to wear and what Peter calls beautiful (Colossians 3:12, 1 Peter 3:4).

I definitely have miles to go, but by God's grace I overlook offenses more than before. Scripture almost makes this sound like we are wearing superhero capes: "He who is slow to anger is better than the mighty; and he that rules his spirit, than he that takes a city" (Proverbs 16:32). And William Penn paints a picture of the caped victor at the end of a hard fought challenge: "He who forgives first wins the laurel." It's a reference to the leafy laurel wreath awarded to the winning athlete in ancient Greece.

So next time you find yourself behind *that* coupon lady in the grocery line, or with a dinner guest who gives you a back-handed, tough-crusty compliment, don your cape—go for the laurel. Be meek. Remember: *It's to your honor to forgive. It's big to give up the last word. Make like a duck. Don't let offenses get under your feathers. Let them roll off like water.* We can't hold onto that anger without it corrupting us. Only God can do that. "And he who sees what is done in secret"—even in the secret of your soft, overlooking heart—"will reward you in the open" (Matthew 6:4).

The meek bank on this.

3. Be Trendy: All things trend toward our good in the Lord.

"We know that for those who love God all things work together for good, for those who are called according to his purpose" (Romans 8:28).

All things means *all things*. All. Things. Annoying drivers. Thoughtless comments. Irritating neighbors. Rebellious children. Clueless friends. All means all. *All* provocations. *All things.* They trend toward good.

Matthew Henry[10] issued a challenge for us sensitive types to find the good in all *things*.

> *There is no provocation given to us at any time, but if it be graciously improved, there is good to be gotten by it. This is a holy and happy way of opposing our adversaries, and resisting evil. It is an ill weed indeed out of which the spiritual bee cannot extract something profitable.*

This has been such a transforming truth in my life. I am learning to trust that the slights and snubs, accidental or intended, that come to me may be the exact provocations God means for my good. Meekness is the bee seeking sweetness in the weeds.

Because if it's not one thing, it's another. *Why do I let my husband's dishwasher loading method bother me so easily? Why do I get annoyed when one friend comes five minutes early and another greets me in an obnoxious sing-songy voice?* These are such small, small things.

When in meekness, we look for the good and *over*look an offense; we adorn the doctrine of our merciful, meek God. We gain victory over those that injure us, and in our meek response, the eyes of our offender's heart may just see Jesus. Meekness is strength put under God's control. It is the taming grace that frees me from the urge to avenge and repay. In other words:

Meekness frees me from the tyranny of me.

Wounds, insults, and misunderstandings are bound to come. How will we meet them? Truly, Henry writes[10]), "It is the evil of [offense] that turns our friends into enemies: but it is the excellency of meekness that it turns our enemies into friends." Will we be that sensitive or will we be like Jesus?

Overlooking offenses, like Jesus, in order to win hearts—this, too, is meek.

FOR FURTHER REFLECTION:

1. Were you a "sensitive" child? On a scale of 1-5, with 1 being oblivious and 5 being hypersensitive, where would you place yourself now?

2. The chapter begins with a line by C.S. Lewis about how we should deal with sensitivity: "be merciless to its first appearance in ourselves." Now that you've read the chapter, do you think he is overstating the case? Why or why not? Similarly, Oswald Chambers wrote, "Self-pity is of the devil." Thinking back, can you recall a time when someone hurt you and it led to self-pity? What happened then?

3. What is the difference between lament and self-pity? How would you tell if you are moving from godly grieving, or lament, to ungodly self-pity? Why would lament be a healthy reaction to hardship and self-pity an unhealthy one?

4. We've seen several examples in this chapter of Jesus Christ being insulted or misunderstood. They are found in Matthew 9:24-25, 9:33-34; 9:11:2-3; 13:21-23, 13:55-57; 16:22-23; Luke 22:61-63. What is striking about Christ's responses?

5. Read Ephesians 4:26-27, 6:11-14 and 2 Corinthians 2:10-11. How could being *that* sensitive leave the door open to the devil's schemes in your life? What is a healthier, more biblical way to deal with offenses and events that make us angry?

6. Being reasonable is the opposite of being "*that* sensitive." Being reasonable goes part and parcel with being meek. Reread Philippians 4:5. Is your reasonable meekness well known? Or do people tiptoe around you, afraid that you'll sulk or cry or punish them in some passive way for speaking?

7. At the end of this chapter, the author shares three truths that help her build "a thicker skin" and a softer heart: 1) *Do unto others by assuming the best.* 2) *It is glorious to overlook an offense.* 3) *Be trendy: All things tend toward our good in the Lord.* Which of these most resonate with you? In what circumstance in your life this week can you practice it?

PRAYER OF RESPONSE

Dear Lord Jesus, thank you for modeling meekness when others misunderstood, insulted and laughed at you. Thank you that you were always full of grace and truth and you never lashed out in kind or sulked. Please give me the strength to forgive and the reasonable, peaceable wisdom from above that discerns when I should confront and when I should overlook.

Amen.

MORE MEEK

10 - More Meek than Before

Practice these things, immerse yourself in them, so that all may see your progress.

—Paul to Timothy, in 1 Timothy 4:15

"Hey Dad, can we stop here, like last year?" our ten-year-old asked.

As the van slowed, my heart raced.

"Sure, guys. Let's stop," was my husband's chipper reply.

Breathe in. Love is patient. Breathe out. Love is kind. Breathe in. Don't insist. Breathe out. Act meek.

By the time I pushed that third breath out, our van had veered off the highway and on to Sanibel Causeway Island A. Mind you, this was not a beautiful Sanibel Island beach. It was however the exact site of an ugly family showdown one year prior. Last year emotional fireworks erupted when, after 22 hours in the car, this let's-get-there-already mom pushed back against laid-back let's-smell-the-roses dad.

The Sanibel Causeway is the super-long bridge that connects the mainland to the island. For us, it represented the final three miles in our 1,500 mile trek from Wisconsin to Sanibel. For perspective, imagine grilling out on a Friday night. The table is set and the meat is just starting to sizzle when the grill tank runs dry. Deciding to stop at Island A *to play* equates to leaving the deck and dinner's scent to drive to town at the peak of rush hour for a propane refill. It. Was. Painful.

While love is patient and Jesus was meekness in the flesh, I was neither that day. Actually, I am generally neither. Truth be told, there was nary a naturally meek or self-less bone in my body that day. I preferred my get-there-and-get-settled agenda to their leisurely enjoy-the-journey-meander. But I was working on this meekness thing. I wanted to be more meek. And this was a test. So, I decided right then and there that stopping at Island A for a measly 20 minutes after driving 22 hours could *not* steal my joy. I would not grumble.

> If God commands it, we can do it. Just because you have never done it before is no proof that you cannot do it starting today.
>
> —*Andrée Seu Peterson*[2]

MEEKNESS GROWS SLOWLY AFTER BEING SO WILD FOR SO LONG

Well, *that* didn't happen!. Last year, *I* failed the test. Commander Mom, the Meekness Anti-type, donned her Mrs. Business hat. "Come on, you guys, let's go or we'll miss the sunset on the beach. You know I love sunset on the beach and we only have seven. Let's go—now. I said move." My spirit was provoked so, un-meek, steamroller-esque. Which isn't really all that surprising—I've been coping this way for a long time.

Taming is supernatural.

> *"Some of 'em you jest can't gentle. Not after they've lived wild. Only he youngsters is worth botherin' about, so far as the gentlin' goes."*

That's a quote from Grandpa Beebe about the wild ponies of Chincoteague[3]. Phantom was one of those. She never gentled, like Grandpa's Kickin' Jack. Neither ever got tamed or accustomed to their master's hand. Those ponies were not meek.

But thank God, no matter how long we've lived wild, we can be.

If the last five chapters left you feeling less than a meek-master, you are not alone. No one, I repeat, no one is *naturally* loving, joyful, peaceful, or meek. These qualities are fruit that the Holy Spirit produces in us. It's important to remember this so we don't lose heart when we fail. Christians are lifelong learners.

While there's still life in us, there's hope. Because if God commands it, we can do it. He equips us with all we need to grow.

Peter said, "Grow in the grace and knowledge of Jesus" (2 Peter 3:18), and Paul wrote, "Practice these things, immerse yourself in them, so that all may see your progress" (1 Timothy 4:15). John said, "Everyone who practices righteousness is righteous" (1 John 3:7b).

Practice, progress and *grow.* These words teach us that we haven't arrived. Both my sons practice piano, my husband makes progress in grooming our woodland trails, I grow in the craft of writing. But we must do the thing if we want to improve. There will be wrong notes, more sprouting sumac, and continuous revising. But the important thing is that we learn, we practice, and we grow.

Then we won't say "I *should have been.*" I should have been more like Jesus, I should have been more meek. I love that line in *Pride and Prejudice*[4] where old Lady Catherine says, "There are few people in England, I suppose, who have more true enjoyment of music than myself, or a better natural taste. If I had ever learnt, I should have been a great proficient." Not us. We don't settle for "should have been," at least not when it comes to maturing Spirit fruit.

So even though harshness and impatience plague me, or worry or resentment plague you, we don't have to give way. We *practice* righteousness and *grow* in meekness and we do make progress. Christians are dynamic, ever transforming from glory to glory (2 Corinthians 3:18). We are not content with the status quo.

YOU DON'T HAVE TO SETTLE

Author Andrée Seu Peterson[5] takes static Christians to task.

> *If God commands it, we can do it. Just because you have never done it before is no proof that you cannot do it starting today. ...Be the first on your block. "Let God be true though every man a liar." We don't have to settle. In Christ, abiding in His Word, we grow. We progress. We bear the fruit of righteousness. We don't say, "This is just how I am and this is how I always will be."*

God's children grow. They change. And they change the way they see the world. They see that it is God who works in us, "both to will and to work for his good pleasure" (Philippians 2:13). One of his good purposes for us is that we be more meek. In fact, theologian Sinclair Ferguson[6] has gone so far as to say, "I am not progressing as a Christian believer unless I am becoming increasingly meek."

But *progress* can be a delicate subject. When someone tells me that I'm making progress in my writing it means my writing skills have room for improvement. When someone tells me they've noticed that I'm more patient it suggests that they have noticed my impatience. When others note progress, as they should, it is evidence of God's grace, but it also means there was room to grow. So when Paul tells Timothy (1 Timothy 4:15) "Be diligent in these matters; give yourself wholly to them, so that everyone may see your progress," Timothy's smile may have been half cringe. When a friend told me last week, "You're more go-with-the-flow," I smile-winced.

We don't have to stay how we are. We don't have to settle. Our past experience—as in my first Island A failure—does not need to dictate our present reality. Meekness is possible. Matthew Henry noted[7], wherever "there is true grace, there is a disposition to strive against, and strength in some measures to conquer that distemper." We can make progress. We can seek meekness.

But our enemy would have us believe that we can't change. He'd deceive us into thinking that impatient, or worrier, or grumbling me is the me I will always be. That's a big fat lie. We must "encourage one another, as long as it's called today, not to be hardened by the deceitfulness of sin" (Hebrews 3:13). And one of the big deceptions about sin is that we're stuck where we are: *I'm just impatient. He's always had a bad temper. She's just that way.* We must call out that lie.

Because the truth is, we are *no longer slaves to sin* (Romans 6:6). We can change. So by grace, as we pulled off the highway and onto Island A, minutes shy of Sanibel Island, I *put on meekness.* By some miracle of taming grace, I ignored the fading sun and followed the boys onto the sand. I set my way aside, submitted my cause and passed that test and saw how the Lord had grown meekness in me.

The Island A test seemed like such a small thing. But it was a foundation brick in my quest for meekness.. You can probably point to far bigger steps of faith. But I share it so that you know that spiritual growth, like physical growth, happens little by little. Brick by brick. We don't see it overnight. We grow by baby steps in obedience and inches over days and months and years. Unlike the inevitable physical growth, spiritual growth demands our cooperation. Our effort. We talk back to our resistant selves. We don't let past failures dictate present obedience. It's not one and done, all or nothing, meek or not meek. "For a righteous man falls seven times, and rises again" (Proverbs 24:16). When we lash out at 8 a.m., we dare not give away the day. Strengthened by grace, we get up and keep on keeping on.

We know that we don't *arrive* at perfection until we reach heaven. We *are being* sanctified. Being remade in the likeness of Jesus takes time. Sanctification is progressive. It is ongoing, gradual, and unfolding. We each grow at a different pace and from a different starting place. We must not compare our growth with others' growth. As my mama reminds me, "Stay in your own lane."

WHEN WE SHOULD, AND SHOULDN'T, COMPARE

C.S. Lewis[8] was asked once about comparing "niceness" among people. He wasn't talking specifically about meekness per se, but his answer is so helpful to us who are tempted to compare our growth to others.

> *Take the case of a sour old maid, who is a Christian, but cantankerous. On the other hand, take some pleasant and popular fellow, but who has never been to Church. Who knows how much more cantankerous the old maid might be if she were not a Christian, and how much more likable the nice fellow might be if he were a Christian? You can't judge Christianity simply by comparing the product in those two people; you would need to know what kind of raw material Christ was working on in both cases.*

We simply do not know the raw material. So we dare not compare ourselves with others. Paul made that plain when he wrote to the Corinthian church: "We do not dare to classify or compare ourselves with some who commend themselves. When they measure themselves by themselves and compare themselves with themselves, they are not wise" (2 Corinthians 10:12). Playing the comparison game in spiritual growth is unwise.

In the last chapter of John, the Resurrected Lord is walking along the shore with Peter. The beloved apostle John is behind them.

> *When Peter saw him, he asked, "Lord, what about him?" Jesus answered, "If I want him to remain alive until I return, what is that to you? You must follow me.* (John 21:21-22)

Following Jesus, *every* Christian will make progress and grow. So while we are told not to compare ourselves with others to evaluate our progress, we are called to compare ourselves with *ourselves* (1 Timothy 4:15). This is how we see growth. If a friend or sister, a husband or wife compared you now with the you they knew two or 22 years ago, would they see progress? Could they observe growth? Are you less cantankerous and more kind; less pushy and more patient? Do you worry less and trust more? Are you more responsive to God's hand?

Maybe those are hard questions. Maybe there has been slow growth. In this area of meekness my growth has been two steps forward and one step back. In these times, C.S. Lewis[8] encourages my heart.

> *If you are a poor creature, poisoned by a wretched upbringing in some house full of vulgar jealousies and senseless quarrels [...] do not despair. He knows all about it. You are one of the poor whom He blessed. He knows what a wretched machine you are trying to drive. Keep on. Do what you can. One day (perhaps in another world, but perhaps far sooner than that) he will fling it on the scrap-heap and give you a new one. And then you may astonish us all—not least yourself: for you have learned your driving in a hard school.*

We all learn meekness in a hard school, no matter what car we're driving. This strong, taming grace does not come by coasting along.

Sanibel Island Causeway A was a sort of meekness mile marker for me. It allowed me to see my own spiritual growth. It allowed me to compare me then to me a year later. By God's grace, I saw growth.

It might be slow going, but are you growing? Can you look back to a time this week when by grace you put off resentment, or worry or impatience, and breathed in meekness? We don't grow at the same rate and we drive different cars, but with eyes fixed on Christ, we will progress in the race marked out for us.

Here are two takeaways for us who want to grow more meek:

1. **Celebrate the progress you see.** I know it's risky to call this sort of progress out. After all, it implies that there was room for growth. But when we celebrate these baby-step successes, we're not celebrating ourselves. We're celebrating, "for it is God who works in you both to will and to work for his good pleasure" (Philippians 4:13).

2. **Don't give up if progress is slow.** Direction over perfection; growth over arrival. We don't compare ourselves with others, but we also don't ignore our failures. We don't blame bad experiences or our temperament or how we were brought up. We don't give up because we know the Father "knows our frame" (Psalm 103:14). Don't forget, what he does to us, he does for us. Meekness knows that God gives us what we need.

We follow Jesus. For wild ponies, following won't feel natural. Meekness isn't natural. It will feel like a stretch. It will feel like stepping onto shadowy

Causeway Island A when the splendid sun is setting miles away on a spectacular Sanibel beach. That's what growth is.

It's what Anonymous said:

I'm not what I was.

I'm not what I should be.

And I'm not what I will be.

But glory to God, all God's children grow up into Jesus. Fast or slow, we all grow more meek.

FOR FURTHER REFLECTION:

1. In this chapter, the focus shifts from biblical "meek masters" to our own spiritual growth. The author describes her experience at Causeway Island A as a sort of "meekness mile marker," because it was a moment in time when she could look back and measure her own growth. Can you think of your own "meekness mile marker"—a more submissive, more trusting response to a hard situation?

2. We might find ourselves making excuses for our lack of meekness. They might sound like "It's hard to be gentle after being wild for so long," or "If I'd have learned, I *would have been* a great proficient." If you're honest, what reasons, if any, have you given to excuse yourself from spiritual growth?

3. Peter said, "Grow in the grace and knowledge of Jesus" (2 Peter 3:18), and Paul wrote, "Practice these things, immerse yourself in them, so that all may see your progress" (1 Timothy 4:15). John said, "Everyone who practices righteousness is righteous" (1 John 3:7b). How do these verses explain our part in spiritual growth?

4. Compared with the you your friends knew two or 22 years ago, are you more meek than you were? For example, are you less irritable, more kind? Are you less resentful, more gentle? Are you less pushy, more patient? Slower to anger, faster to forgive? Fill in the blanks: "I'm less _____ and more _____ than I was _____ years ago."

5. Read Romans 6:1-14 about being slaves to Christ and not to sin. Verse 6 says, "For we know that our old self was crucified with him so that the body ruled by sin might be done away with, that we should no longer be slaves to sin." How can you use this truth when you are tempted to respond with "the old ways" to difficult people and hard circumstances?

6. Do you think Sinclair Ferguson is overstating when he observed, "I am not progressing as a Christian believer unless I am becoming increasingly meek." Why or why not?

7. Review Paul's words in 2 Corinthians 10:12. Why is it dangerous to compare our spiritual growth to that of others? Do you agree that this sort of comparison tends to leave us feeling either discouraged or smug? To whom should we compare ourselves?

PRAYER OF RESPONSE

Dear Lord Jesus, thank you that what you command you also enable. You call me to learn meekness and you work in me to become more meek. Help me to avoid minimizing "the day of small things." Help me to rejoice and press on toward the great goal of knowing you. Thank you that you are at work in me to will and to act according to your good purpose. Amen.

11 - Tending to Meekness

Meekness is not a native fruit of the human heart. It is an exotic fruit of heaven.

—Corrie ten Boom[1]

But grow in the grace and knowledge of our Lord and Savior Jesus Christ. To him be the glory both now and to the day of eternity. Amen.

—2 Peter 3:18

I warned you. This meekness business is not for the faint of heart. The taming of the selfish soul, this breaking of the strong will is not for wimps. You've probably been saying, "Abigail, this is so hard to do. Those meek masters are so unnatural." You are absolutely right. Getting used to God's hand is not natural. A meek response is impossible without the Holy Spirit's working in us.

We know that meekness is a fruit of the Spirit. It comes from really knowing and abiding in God's love (John 15:9). John Calvin[3] clearly connected meekness with loving God. It is loving God, he says, that allows us "to see his hand in everything: to own him as the governor of the world, and the director of providence."

It was this view that allowed Joseph to forgive his brothers, Moses to calmly receive opposition and take "no" for a final answer, David to repent with Nathan and to stop short of clobbering Shimei as he cursed. It is what enabled Job to worship when God took away and empowered Paul to give grace when his friends deserted him in Rome and to see God's appointment when he was imprisoned and on trial alone.

Seeing God's hand is what helps me to see past the big and small disappointments in my life rather than wallow in self-pity or lash out in wounded pride. When I bite my tongue and don't set the record straight, when I smile at the train crossing gates, this is God's power in my weakness. Yes, the Lord is upright, in whose strength I stand and sit and wait. We simply cannot grow more meek without setting our gaze beyond the earthly second causes to the invisible hand of God.

But we must put meekness on. Colossians 3:12 calls us to get dressed in meekness. We wouldn't dream of leaving our house without getting dressed. It would be criminal to go to work dressed only in underwear. So we must intentionally "get dressed" daily in meekness. That might be as simple as a short prayer before we roll out of bed:

> Following Christ and His example is not easy, but is possible through the power of the Holy Spirit. Living the Christian life without the Lord in your life is impossible, but we can do all things through Christ. It is the Lord who enables us to be meek and will reward those who are meek with a great inheritance when He returns.
>
> *–Rod Mattoon*[2]

"Help me be more meek today for the glory of Jesus. Amen."

Because we don't need to learn a new thing every day, it might mean repeating the same meek work day after day. We should have days when we allow what is in us to swell up until it overflows. Living the gentle strength requires we let meekness swell. We need to let the word of Christ dwell in us richly. We need to abide and obey.

CAN YOU CHOOSE MEEKNESS OR PRODUCE SPIRIT FRUIT?

Meekness is a fruit of the Spirit. But have you noticed that each virtue on the list of Spirit fruit (Galatians 5:22-23) has corresponding calls to *put on*, and to live out, each quality. We are called, for example, to "put on love" (Colossians 3:14), "to be joyful always" (1 Thessalonians 5:16), to "pursue self-control" (2 Timothy 2:22), "to make every effort to add to our faith goodness" (2 Peter 1:5-8), and to "clothe yourselves with meekness" (Colossians 3:12). Yes, they are fruits, but they are also commands.

So, can we simply choose to be meek?

Well, yes and no. We can choose to overlook an offense. We can choose to give thanks rather than grumble. We can choose to trust that God's loving hand was behind the hard thing that happened.

But it's important we remember that these choices aren't made in isolation. Pastor and author Benjamin Vrbicek[4] explains that:

> [the choice to be unoffendable] is an interlocking one determined by our answers to a host of other questions. To use an analogy, is the choice to run a marathon just one choice? Well, yes and no. To be sure, it's a choice, but it's not a choice made in isolation from other choices about diet, sleep, training, and rest.

The decisions we make to respond with submission to God, his Word, and his people—the myriad meek responses we make–are empowered by the Spirit and carried out in faith. "Whatever a man sows, he will reap in return" (Galatians 6:7). In other words, what we feed grows.

We received the Holy Spirit when we first put our trust in Christ. "Did you receive the Spirit by works of the law or by hearing with faith?" (Galatians 3:2). Faith is the channel by which believers are united to Christ, and the Spirit flows into us by virtue of our union with Christ through faith. So meekness, just like love, joy, peace, patience and kindness, are produced in us by the Spirit through our faith in Jesus Christ. These "works of faith" are like spiritual muscles that need to be exercised because, in a real sense, faith is not faith until it is put to the test.

So, how do we exercise our meek muscles? What can we do to cooperate with the Spirit as this fruit grows?

HELPING MEEKNESS GROW

Thankfully, Scripture is full of practical advice. We glean from Scripture the means of grace that God provides and we apply those means in our daily lives. We can, for example, heed God's words to his willful hard-hearted people, people he would harness and tame for his glory.

> Sow for yourselves righteousness; reap steadfast love; break up your fallow ground, for it is the time to seek the LORD, that he may come and rain righteousness upon you. (Hosea 10:12)

We break up the hard soil of our hearts by pursuing meekness so that the Spirit's fruit can grow. While we don't want to risk mixing metaphors here, we can say that meekness requires both. It is a fruit and a pursuit. The pursuit—getting the ground ready to receive—takes muscle. We are fight the good fight of faith (1 Timothy 6:12). We make every effort to supplement our faith (2 Peter 1:5). As God's chosen ones, holy and beloved, we put on meekness (Colossians 3:12). That's our part. Our pursuit. We must seek meekness.

Which means we are not passive. When it comes to meekness, we don't say, "Let go and let God." No, we seek to grow more meek. But we only work out his strong grace because God is already at work in us, "both to will and to act, according to his good pleasure" (Philippians 2:12-13). That is the only way that we can grow in the taming grace of meekness.

At the end of his second letter, Peter calls us to "grow in the grace and knowledge of our Lord and Savior Jesus Christ" (2 Peter 3:18). The word "grow" is such a stabilizing word. It prevents two great dangers—stagnation and perfectionism. The word *grow* keeps us from thinking that we are stuck, that we'll never change, that we'll always be how we are today. At the same time, the word *grow* guards us against thinking that, this side of heaven, we will fully arrive. It keeps us grounded and humble. Because if growth is possible, it means we're not yet perfected. We are ever arriving.

Charles Spurgeon[5] uses this garden imagery as well:

> *Oh, to have one's soul under heavenly cultivation, no wilderness, but a garden of the Lord, walled around by grace, planted by instruction, visited by love, weeded by heavenly discipline, and guarded by divine power. One's soul thus favored is prepared to yield fruit to the glory of God.*

There are countless ways to pursue that "heavenly" heart cultivation and help meekness grow. Let's start with these.

8 WAYS TO HELP MEEKNESS GROW

1. Stay Near People Who Rub You Wrong.

If our habit is to walk out when someone upsets us, how can we possibly grow more meek? If all our friends are "Yes" friends, who don't dare to show us our blindsides, we will be spiritually stunted. "Rather, speaking the truth in love, we are to grow up in every way into him who is the head, into Christ" (Ephesians 4:15). Meekness is the "cement of society, the bond of Christian community" Matthew Henry wrote[6]. We must make allowances.

Colossians 3:13 says, "Bear with each other." If it were easy to coexist, and if it were easy to share and hear truth in love, Paul wouldn't have used the word "bear." It means to patiently bear hard circumstances and difficult people. Recall that meekness is submission to God's will, his Word and his people. Yielding to God's will and his Word are absolute. Please note that there are obvious exceptions in the bounds of our submission to his people, including, but not limited to, disobedience and abuse. Those cases are not part of this application

If we zoom out just a bit on that text we'll see that submitting to one another is one of four marks of being Spirit-filled that Paul provides in Ephesians 5:19. "Be filled with the Spirit" is the main command. Then Paul offers four marks of that filling—"speaking, singing, giving thanks," and then the last one, "submitting to one another out of reverence for Christ." Submission to others in the family of faith, then, is evidence of the Spirit at work within us. Since we've already seen that meekness is a fruit of the Spirit (Galatians 5:23), this should come as no surprise.

Application: This is huge. So many of my rough, self-righteous edges have been rubbed off by staying in committed relationships with folks at my church with whom I disagree. Friends who love to sing sentimental songs rather than strong hymns, and prefer different models of Christian education than I do. We've talked through those and I haven't been persuaded on these things. Nor has the Lord led me to leave. Which means I have a choice. Stick around and submit, bad mouth and divide, or walk away. Only one way tends toward meekness. When we remain in places or with people we would not have chosen, we have prime opportunities to grow more meek.

2. Moderate your expectations of others.

"We all stumble in many ways" (James 3:2). Remembering God's trend is toward use of this for our good. Stumbles tend toward meekness. In many things we offend. Recall also that our "God knows our frame. He knows we are dust" (Psalm 103:14). If the perfect God has this sort of sympathy for us, we ought also to deal with others this way. We must remember that every single Christian is a sinner *in the process of recovery*. Every single believer, author Mike Emlet[7] observes, is at once a saint, a sinner, and a sufferer. My friend Terre says it this way: "We tend to judge others by what we see, but to judge ourselves by our heart." The meek learn to give others the benefit of the doubt. They begin by assuming pure heart motives.

We bear patiently with the hurtful actions of others and we deal gently with their failures, knowing that we are no better. We know that given different circumstances we just might commit all sorts of sins that don't tempt us now. Offenses abound. Which means that opportunities to grow more meek do too. Proverbs 19:11 says, "A person's wisdom yields patience; it is to one's glory to overlook an offense."

Application: "Mom, do you think they forgot my birthday?" That, from our 12-year-old birthday boy as he sorted through the stack of mail. The card from a special aunt and uncle was nowhere to be found. No text, no call, no card, no song. He lowered his head, closed his eyes. As much as I wanted to, I couldn't stop the hurt. Yet meekness demands we assume the best and look past the worst. "Aunt Tina and Uncle Todd are really busy this month, Bud. I know they love you." This is not to deny the place for grief, or "truth in love" confrontation, only to say that in meekness our toggle is set to overlook.

3. Practice gratitude, starting with God's patience and forgiveness.

Matthew Henry[8] suggests we ask ourselves: "If God were to be as angry at me for my offenses against him as I am at others for their offenses against me, where would I be? We all have reason to say that Jesus Christ is very meek or else we, who have provoked him so much and so often would have been in hell long ago." In 1 Timothy 1:15-16 Paul says, "Here is a trustworthy saying that deserves full acceptance: Christ Jesus came into the world to save sinners—of whom I am the worst. But for that very reason I was shown mercy so that Christ Jesus might display his immense patience as an example for those who would believe in him." The meek know, "There, but for the grace of God go I."

God has shown massive mercy and great patience to each one of us. We don't deserve an ounce of his grace. Until God made us alive in Christ, "we were by nature objects of wrath" (Ephesians 2:3). So we thank God often for his mercy toward us and we are on the lookout for God's grace in the lives of those who are hardest to love. Whether a teenager or husband, in-laws or boss, the meek actively seek in them evidence of God's work, and give him thanks. It might mean giving God thanks for the smallest of things—a smile from a hurting friend or a one-word text from a prodigal child.

Application: Un-meek me gets irritable when people don't reply quickly to my texts and emails. But more-meek me quotes Herbert the Snail, who sings, "Remember, remember, that God is patient too. And think of all the times when others have to wait for you." It's true. I make others wait. Recently, I was beside myself to know I'd let a text from a friend sit for over a week. When a friend didn't reply to not one but four texts last week, by God's strong grace I did this. I assumed the best and forgave, "forgiving each other just as in Christ God forgave you" (Ephesians 4:32b). That was enough.

4. Go slow in evaluating others and assume the best until you know the worst.

Sometimes, Henry noted[9], "the children of men are more than ordinarily provoking, and then the children of God have more than commonly need of meekness." James 1:19, "Let every person be quick to listen, slow to speak and slow to anger." The meek don't assume motives, but they do assume the best about others, at least until they see the worst. They are slow to anger.

We must remember that "others" includes God. Jeremiah Burroughs'[10] advice is timeless.

> *Have good thoughts of God and make good interpretations of his dealings toward you. It is very hard to live comfortably and cheerfully among friends when one makes harsh interpretations of the words and actions of others....A primary way to help keep comfort and contentment in our hearts is to make good interpretations of God's dealings with us.*

Application: In the second game of the Little League season, our son got parked in the outfield, with little fielding opportunity. "Were the coaches following rotation protocol?" this Tiger Mom wanted to ask. This Tiger Mom assumed the worst. The Spirit convinced me to wait. "What is said and done in haste is likely to need repentance."[11] Sure enough, the next game he was rotated to pitcher. His arm was well rested.

5. Make friends with meek people.

Someone said that *we are the sum of our five best friends*. Proverbs 22:24 says, "Make no friendship with a man given to anger, lest you learn his ways." Conversely, Proverbs 13:22 says, "He who walks with the wise grows wise." Do you have meek friends? Do you have friends who help you trust God, or encourage you to hold your tongue, who ask you to take a breath? Matthew Henry[12] wrote, "We grow like those with whom we converse; therefore, let the meek in the land be our best friends."

We need to see meekness applied. We need to see it lived before our eyes. My son watched YouTube videos to learn how to fold clothes. I took a course from a graphic artist to learn graphic art. We need to hear suffering friends say that they trust God. We need to see naturally strong, powerful friends submit and yield for Christ's sake. We need to see how it looks in the flesh. If you want to be a writer, you must write and hang out with other writers. If you want to be a cook, you must cook and saute with other chefs. If you want to be more meek, you've got to be with meek people who pursue meekness. You've got to see the copy. "Imitate me," Paul said, "as I imitate Christ" (1 Corinthians 1:11). First we see Jesus in his word, but then we must have friends who live out meekness before our eyes.

Application: Start your own #meekgeek Bible study or life group. Use this book as your guide. Cultivate closeness with people who love you enough, who are committed enough, to speak truth to you (Ephesians 4:15). Don't settle for "Yes men" friends. Choose friends who are growing more meek and they will help you see meek. Meek like Jesus.

6. Rejoice with those who rejoice. Take pleasure in others' pleasure.

"Anybody can sympathise with the sufferings of a friend, but it requires a very fine nature to sympathise with a friend's success." Not a paragon of virtue, Oscar Wilde[13] still saw this right. But what he called a "very fine nature," I call a "new creation." No natural man can do this. Only the new creation can. It's only by grace through faith in Christ that I'm able to set aside hurt or disappointment or pride to rejoice with those who rejoice—especially in things I want that aren't mine. It takes massive meekness.

But it is what we're called to do. Romans 12:15 says, "Rejoice with those who rejoice and weep with those who weep." It is supernatural to say, "Our three bedrooms are enough for us, but I'm glad they could afford that 5,000 square-foot house." Or, "My son is really struggling now, but thank God my friend's son is doing well." But if we share joy, as C.H. Spurgeon[14] preached, "your joy will be unfailing. The meek-spirited man is glad to know that other people are happy even when he's not because their happiness is his happiness."

Application: "One more pumpkin in the pumpkin patch," was how my cousin's pregnancy announcement came, in the same season my own womb ached for fruit (Proverbs 30:16). When a friend said she started her dream job last week with the words "It's a perfect fit," I swallowed hard. My job is not a perfect fit. Especially not this week. But God's taming grace is strong, so I wrote, "Congrats on your precious gift!" I leaned in to ask, "Could you show me some of your work?" Then she took me to an amazing website she'd built. It was a perfect fit for her passion and skill. Then by some miracle of grace, joy welled up in me and I really did rejoice.

7. Walk daily in fellowship with Jesus Christ.

We become what we behold. In 2 Corinthians 3:18, Paul says "beholding the glory of the Lord, are being transformed into the same image from one degree of glory to another." We've got to see more meek to be more meek. Which takes us back to Christ's delightful invite: "Take my yoke upon you and learn from me, for I am meek and humble of heart; and you will find rest for yourselves" (Matthew 11:29, New American Bible). The only way we can possibly be meek and humble like Jesus is to share his yoke. It's almost as if his meekness rubs off on us as we pull life's loads beside him, who "daily bears our burdens," (Psalm 68:19).

Since Jesus doesn't walk the earth today, it means we must spend time in His Word. It's our way of "sitting at his feet" and listening like Mary did (Luke 10:39). We must choose the better thing "which cannot be taken from us." We cannot allow ourselves to be distracted away from time with Jesus, even with good things.

Application: I'm not immune from iPhone distraction. I know what it is to drift so long that the pizza burns and the sink overflows. So, by grace, I make the practice of leaving my phone far away when I spend time in daily devotions. Sometimes, I'd rather listen to a podcast or post my own content. I've found that French saying to be apt here: *Appetite comes with eating.* So, I keep eating, reading, and abiding. As I yoke myself this way to the meek and lowly Jesus day by day; slowly, slowly, he makes me more meek.

8. Anticipate all that God has promised.

Pastor Erwin Lutzer[15] said, "The meek look at life through a telescope, not a microscope." I think he meant that the meek know how to zoom out. Today's news doesn't have to take our breath away. We know that God will win, that "though the wrong seems often strong," as the hymn puts it, "God is the ruler yet." The meek have this promise and God is always faithful to every promise he makes. Therefore, the meek can "sit loose" to this world. They have their hands open to receive what God sends. When earthly hopes and comforts crumble around us, we can bank on our future inheritance—and rejoice now.

"Blessed are the meek, for they will inherit the earth." The meek know the third beatitude by heart and look forward to their inheritance. In 1 Peter 1:4 we read that there is an "inheritance kept in heaven for you," and in 2 Peter 3:13, "According to his promise we are looking for new heavens and a new earth, in which righteousness dwells." Ephesians 1:14 says the Holy Spirit is, "the pledge of our inheritance." So we await the day when "the creation itself will be liberated from its bondage to decay and brought into the freedom and glory of the children of God" (Romans 8:21). Leaning into these promises, the meek see life through a telescope.

Application: I love sunshine but I live in a rather dark house deep in a hickory forest. While I thrive on bright light, I must turn on indoor lights at mid-day. How do I cope? I go for walks a lot. But I also grab my spiritual telescope, and tell myself this truth: The best is yet to come, because "the meek will inherit the earth."

"Seek the Lord, you meek of the earth; seek meekness" (Zephaniah 2:3, New King James Version). Oh, yes, the meek keep seeking to grow more meek.

FOR FURTHER REFLECTION

1. Biblically, meekness is both a fruit of the Spirit and a virtue we are called to put on. How do the following texts explain the relationship between human effort and divine enabling in spiritual growth?

   - Philippians 2:12-13

   - Colossians 1:29

   - 1 Corinthians 15:10

2. Christians are called to "grow in the grace and knowledge of our Lord and Savior Jesus Christ" (2 Peter 3:18). How might the term "growth" keep you from the twin dangers of spiritual stagnation and perfectionism?

3. Colossians 3:13 says, "Bear with each other." How can a meek outlook change your perspective on the irritating, extra-grace-required people in your life? How can it affect your perspective on committed church membership? Do you assume the best about others? What about God—do you "make good interpretations of his dealing with you?" What would that look like lived out today?

4. Reread 1 Timothy 1:15-16. How can we imitate Paul's gratitude for God's patience and forgiveness? How might that help us become more meek?

5. List your five closest friends. What can you say about their meekness? Are they copies you want to imitate?

6. *We become what we behold.* Ultimately, the best way to become more meek is to spend time with Jesus. Read Luke 10:38-42, the familiar story about Mary and Martha. What can you do this week to "choose the good thing" that will not be taken from you?

7. Which of the seven ways to cultivate meekness was most convincing to you? What practical application can you make in response?

PRAYER OF RESPONSE

Spirit of Jesus, will you please make me more like Christ, so that I shine before others as I reflect your glory. I echo the church father[15] who prayed, "The more you do in me and by me, humble me the more; keep me meek, lowly, and always ready to give you honor." Thank you for giving grace to the humble.

Amen.

12 - The Meek Inherit the Land

Those who are of a patient and contented spirit are willing to put up with little honor here below; they can bear injuries without resentment; they are not ready to take offense. They are never losers in the long run. One day they will "reign on the earth."

-J.C. Ryle[1]

Blessed are the meek, for they shall inherit the earth.

—Jesus, in Matthew 5:5

For they shall inherit the earth. To write a whole book on meekness and neglect this fantastic promise would be a travesty. Because the Lord Jesus himself made this promise to motivate and empower our meekness. Because "the quietness and openness and vulnerability of meekness... goes against all that we are by our sinful nature," John Piper[3] writes. By now I hope we feel it in our bones: meekness requires supernatural strength.

To forgive, absorb insults and return good for evil, to accept "no" with grace, commit our cause to God and patiently wait for him to act—these take divine power. To submit to God, His Word, and his imperfect people requires immense inner strength. It is a power that comes when we have been trained by God's discipline and grow accustomed to His hand (cf. Hebrews 12:11). This strength is not something we conjure up deep inside.

So what is our power source? Where do we get the strength to be meek?

THE POWER SOURCE FOR MEEKNESS

The source of our strength is *divine* power. But the activating connection *between* our lived out meekness and divine power is knowing and trusting the promises of God. We are the light bulbs; God is the distant generator of electricity; and the Holy Spirit that enables us to know him and his promises are the wires that carry the power.

Peter makes that link explicit:

> We cannot see the world as God means it in the future, save as our souls are characterized by meekness. In meekness, we are its only inheritors. Meekness alone makes the spiritual retina pure to receive God's things as they are, mingling with them neither imperfection nor impurity.
>
> —George MacDonald[2]

> *His divine power has granted to us all things that pertain to life and godliness, through the knowledge of him who called us to his own glory and excellence, by which he has granted to us his precious and very great promises. (2 Peter 1:3-4a)*

The Beatitudes are meant to encourage us to act like the Kingdom citizens we are. Each one contains a promise meant to motivate us: the merciful are promised mercy, mourners are promised comfort, the meek are promised the earth. All are meant to strengthen our resolve to put on the meekness of Christ (cf. Colossians 3:12, Romans 13:14, 2 Corinthians 10:1). While our natural selves would demand our rights, defend every wrong, or retaliate in anger, Jesus says, "Trust me, you will get it all."

The strength to be meek comes when we assure our hearts that the world *will* be—and, in some ways, *already* is ours. This is the perspective Paul wanted to impress on Christians in Corinth. They weren't struggling with meekness per se, but with its flipside, pride.

> *For all things are yours, whether Paul or Apollos or Cephas or the world or life or death or the present or the future, all are yours; and you are Christ's; and Christ is God's.* (1 Corinthians 3:21)

Don't boast, he explained, because the world is yours. "Why not rather suffer wrong? Why not rather be defrauded?" (1 Corinthians 6:7b). It will all be yours.

It's as if Paul was saying, "C'mon, you guys! You don't need to brag about your new shoes when your father owns the whole shoe factory." We don't need to insist that every wrong is made right this side of heaven, because God has made us heirs of the whole world. In Christ Jesus, all things are ours. "He who did not spare his own Son but gave him up for us all, will he not also along with him freely give us all things?" (Romans 8:32). The meek lean into this power-packed promise and believe that "those who seek the Lord lack no good thing" (Psalm 34:10).

In Christ, all things are mine. I must cling to that truth when unfair stings and the envy bug bites. That happened not too long ago when I walked into a friend's big, sunny house—twice the square footage as our little house in the big woods—and again later that day when a friend described her seaside vacation.

"If not now, then in the life to come, it will all be yours, child."

Spiritual hopes for this earth also tempt me. When a friend told me how her teenagers were walking with God and another how her husband supported her desire to quit work "so I can focus on the ministry I love," she said. Meekness tweaked me. When I silently sighed, "God, those are *my* dreams," I heard Him again, *"Seek me, my girl. No good thing."*

But before we move on to look at three distinct ways the meek inherit the earth, we must remember: *inherit* is always only a grace word. No one can demand to be an heir. We are *made* heirs of physical and spiritual wealth by grace (cf. Ephesians 1:11, 1 Peter 1:3-4, Hebrews 9:15). We are not entitled to be God's children or heirs. There is no entitlement here. We don't pay for it, earn it, or deserve this inheritance. The relationship we have with God that makes us co-heirs with Christ is only and ever by grace, through faith. Our inheritance is a gift.

Now that we've got that clear, let's look at three ways the meek inherit *the present* earth.

NOW: PRESENT INHERITANCE FOR THE MEEK

1. The meek inherit that land in the sense that they enjoy what they have.

This side of heaven, we may have little. But it is still the abundant life that Jesus came to bring (John 10:10). Matthew Henry[4] explained that the meek, "inherit the earth in that they are sure to have as much of it as is good for them: as much as will serve to bear them through this world to a better; and who would covet more? Enough is as good as a feast."

Everyday mercies appear as wonders to the meek. The sunset and the rain, the laughter of a child and the breeze on your face, good sleep and sweet tastes—to receive these with wonder is part of the inheriting promise of meekness. The meek have a "pure spiritual retina" that allows them to receive God's things as they are. They are not blind to God's gifts. Thus, as Matthew Henry wrote[5], they "have the most comfortable, undisturbed enjoyment of themselves, their friends, their God." They trace the Father's hand in the common grace that others take for granted.

"The meek man is thankful, happy, and content, and it is contentment that makes life enjoyable," C.H. Spurgeon[6] wrote that in a sermon on the meek. Then he told this story,

> *Here comes a man home to his dinner; he bows his head, and says, "Lord, for what we are about to receive, make us truly thankful," then opens his eyes, and grumbles, "What! Cold mutton again?" His spirit is very different from that of the good old Christian who, when he reached home, found two herrings and two or three potatoes on the table, and pronounced over them this blessing, 'Heavenly Father, we thank you that you have ransacked both earth and sea to find us this food.' His dinner was not as good as the other man's, but he was content with it, and that made it better.*

The meek soul is pleased with whatever God is pleased to give. It is, Henry writes[7], "the continual happiness of [the meek] to make the best of that which is. We inherit the earth as we learn to say, "What pleases God must not displease me." The meek inherit the earth when they enjoy what they have.

2. The meek inherit the land in that they can enjoy even what they do not own.

I enjoy gardens and pools and boats. But, apart from a few patches of shade-loving flowers, I don't own any of them. Yet I relish summertime in my parents' huge gardens, my friend's ski boat, and another friend's pool. I don't own the garden, pool, or boat. Yet I sure enjoy them.

Pastor Kent Hughes[8] explains that the meek are able to enjoy their inheritance now because their lives are "free from the tyranny of 'just a little more.' When a gentle spirit caresses their approach to their rights, then they possess all."

Then he offers the 16th-century English angler Izaak Walton as Exhibit A:

> *I could sit there quietly, and look at the waters and see fishes leaping at*

flies of several shapes and colors. Looking down the meadows, I could see a boy gathering lilies and a girl cropping columbines and cowslips.... As I thus sat, enjoying my own happy condition, I did remember what my Saviour said, that the meek inherit the earth.

This kind of enjoyment is not mooching. This is humble, thankful meekness.

I borrow again from Spurgeon[9],

Even the possessions of other men make these people glad. They are like the man who met a mandarin in China covered with jewels, and, bowing to him, said, "Thank you for those jewels." Doing this many times, at last the mandarin asked the cause of his gratitude. "Well," said the poor but wise man, "I thank you that you have those jewels, for I have as good a sight of them as you have; but I have not the trouble of wearing them, putting them on in the morning, taking them off at night, and having a watchman keeping guard over them when I am asleep. I thank you for them; they are as much use to me as they are to you.'

The meek inherit the earth when they freely enjoy what they *don't* own.

3. The meek inherit the earth in that they not only enjoy whatever they have and what others have, but they are also glad that others have been given the gifts they have.

The meek take pleasure in God's gifts to others. When we learn to "rejoice with those who rejoice" (Romans 12:15a) we have a constant source of joy. Admittedly, to celebrate a friend's marriage or pregnancy, when you'd love to be married or pregnant is nothing short of supernatural. To rejoice with a friend who landed your dream job or the book contract you have labored for is massively meek. It is a gift of God. To celebrate like this is to DIGLI.

I'll explain DIGLI, which rhymes with wiggly, in a minute. But first, do you remember the parable of the vineyard owner? He hired workers at 7 a.m., 9 a.m., 12 p.m., and 5 p.m. Then he gave them all the same exact pay. It's in Matthew 20:10-15, and here's how it ends:

Now when those hired first came, they thought they would receive more, but each of them also received a denarius. And on receiving it they grumbled at the master of the house, saying, 'These last worked only one hour, and you have made them equal to us who have borne the burden of the day and the scorching heat.' But he replied to one of them, 'Friend, I am doing you no wrong. Did you not agree with me for a denarius? Take what belongs to you and go. I choose to give to this last worker as I give to you. Am I not allowed to do what I choose with what belongs to me? Or do you begrudge my generosity?"

We read how the guys who worked twelve hours got the same amount as those who worked one hour, and naturally we're stunned. *Really, Jesus? That seems so unfair!* But wise parents and teachers tell their kids: "Fair isn't equal. It's getting what you need." In His wisdom, God deemed that those vastly *unequal* hourly rates were exactly right, because, as author Lief Enger[9] wrote, "Fair is whatever God wants to do."

The parable helps us understand what theologian and author Joe Rigney[10] meant when he said:

"God loves inequality....In terms of gifts, talents, abilities, opportunities, blessings, God is unequally lavish, at least according to our standards, and that's not a bug, it's a feature."

This means that contrary to popular opinion, inequality of gifts does not need a fix. Envy is the "great leveler" that always opposes meekness and always levels down. In other words, envy would have us move the blessing bar down, to the lowest common denominator. *If I can't make a six-figure income, you shouldn't either.* If my kid can't be a champ, yours shouldn't be either. This is not meek. The envious will not inherit the earth.

Which brings us back to the meek who inherit this present earth as they DIGLI. I coined the term in the midst of my own struggle to put on meekness and put off envy and discontent (Colossians 3:5-13). I needed a word to express that generous, free state of heart. DIGLI, you see, is an acronym for:

Delight

In

God's

Lavish

Inequality.

Clearly this is *not* a natural dance or stance. *Only* the meek can dance the DIGLI.

Discontent spreads when we begrudge God's generosity to others. But the meek trust that God is giving us exactly what we need to conform us to the image of Christ — even if it doesn't make sense. But untamed, natural me wants it to make sense now. I want my kids to be invited if *her* kids are invited. I want my husband to get a week off during spring break when it's finally *his* turn. But that's me when I'm untamed and out of my lane.

When her grandkids compare then complain, I can hear my mom say again, "Stay in your own lane." The meek train themselves to do that. They stay in their own lane, and trust God to give what is good, even when it doesn't seem fair.

The meek inherit this present earth as they enjoy their lives, the gifts from others, and the lavish gifts God shares with others.

THEN: FUTURE INHERITANCE FOR THE MEEK

4. Christ's kingdom alone will stand. The meek will dwell in that land.

"There are only two kinds of people in the end," C. S. Lewis wrote[12], "those who say to God, 'Thy will be done,' and those to whom God says, in the end, 'Thy will be done.'" The meek are the first kind. They have been training themselves to say, "Thy will be done." They aren't working to inherit the earth. They are waiting for God to unlock the full inheritance.

"Blessed are the meek, for they will inherit the earth" is the third Beatitude. We find them all in Matthew 5:3-12. As we read them, it's important to know that they are not random statements, but follow a logical order. The first affirms the poor in spirit as those who recognize their spiritual bankruptcy without God. This leads naturally to mourning over their sin, reflected in the second Beatitude. This mourning leads to the meekness that yields to God who forgives those sins, and deals gently with fellow sinners. In this way, the Beatitudes mark all of God's adopted children. They describe the children of faith.

The promise of our future inheritance of the earth is a direct complement to the meek who now for Christ's sake "give ground," and would rather suffer than sin. It makes sense that Jesus would say to the ones who wait patiently for their inheritance—who don't force their way and grasp to get ahead—"If you trust me, I will give you all the riches in the world later."

Pastor Kevin DeYoung says[13], "to be a Christian is to be a 'later' person, to believe that God has things for us later." Which sounds a lot like Psalm 37:9, "Evildoers shall be cut off, but those who wait for the Lord shall inherit the land." In case we missed the point there, two verses later we read, "the meek shall inherit the land." Then a thousand years later, in the third Beatitude, Jesus expands the psalmist's blessing far beyond the sliver of land on the eastern shore of the Mediterranean Sea to the whole wide world. God's people, meek people, will inherit the earth. "But according to his promise we are waiting for new heavens and a new earth in which righteousness dwells" (2 Peter 3:13). Heaven awaits.

"When all earthly forces are overthrown, Christ's kingdom will stand," C.H. Spurgeon wrote.[14] "Nothing is mightier than meekness, and it is the meek who inherit the earth." Rest assured, the "later people,' the patient waiters, will be blessed.

The meek train themselves to wait. They place all things in God's hands and then God places all things back into their hands. That's why Jesus says, "The meek will inherit the earth."

So possess your soul in patience. No one who waits for him will be put to shame (Psalm 25:13). Your inheritance awaits. Rejoice and be glad.

WE WAIT: BETWEEN ALREADY AND NOT YET

Wait for me. I will come back.

I can't remember the title of the book they come from, but I remember the wife who received those words. She was a beautiful Civil War bride whose groom went off to fight just after they married. But the letter said, *Wait for me. I will come back.* She clung to those words.

Four Aprils had passed and the man she loved was *not* back. But she had promised him *'til death do us part.* So she waited and waited and waited. So much time had passed that when a suitor proposed, it didn't seem uncouth. But her beloved had promised, *I will come back.* Lonely and shaken, but resolved to wait, the bride rejected his offer.

Her strength to wait—to hope against hope—was so palpable, I feel it decades later. But now I know that her strength to wait was the self-constraint, and patience-to-wait strength of meekness. This side of heaven, we will *always* be waiting for something. From the countdown until Christmas or graduation, to being married and having children, to waiting for healing and to be home, we are always waiting. The earth is ours already, and not yet.

But God's meek children don't just grin-and-bear-it wait. They wait patiently because they know *for Whom* they wait. They claim David's words for their own, "And now, O Lord, for what do I wait? My hope is in you" (Psalm 39:7). They know that God is worth the wait, and—this is key to meekness—they know that their wait is not wasted, that God is working as we wait, that he is doing a thousand things and we might not even see one.

Maybe the biggest reason the story of the Civil War bride grips me is that I too feel the allure of hope alongside the burden to wait. And I don't like to wait. Mom's childhood warning to me still rings in my ears, *Don't take matters into your own hands, Ab. Wait.*

The 19-century preacher Phillips Brooks[15] was noted for his poise and quiet manner. At times, however, even he became irritable. One day, a friend saw him pacing the floor like a caged lion.

"What's the trouble, Dr. Brooks?" asked the friend.

"The trouble is that I am in a hurry," said Brooks, "but God isn't."

Oh, yes—everyday I feel the weight of this truth: Waiting on God requires massive inner strength. It is the weak, not the meek, who cave. Patience takes tremendous strength. Impatient people are weak.

We are tempted to bow to physical idols when God doesn't act in our time frame. So we eat more chips, drink more wine and scroll down and down. We don't wait long enough or often enough to get comfortable with the hollow, gnawing, no-bow, loose-ends-still-loose discomfort.

The same is true for our souls. God promises reward to those who wait. James said that our patient waiting makes us "mature and complete, lacking nothing" (James 1:4). Because waiting is how we inherit. The meek are those who choose the way of patient faith instead of self-assertion. They don't, to borrow Mom's words again, *take matters into their own hands.* They are later people.

But make no mistake: Patience—waiting for God to act— requires tremendous spiritual strength. "Impatient people are weak," John Piper notes[16], "and therefore dependent on external supports—like schedules that go just right and circumstances that support their fragile hearts." When we threaten and shout and criticize those who make us wait or ruin our plans, we betray our weakness. My tornado outbursts when my plans fall through don't sound weak, but the noise camouflages weakness. Piper again, "Patience demands tremendous inner strength. For the Christian, this strength comes from God, through faith and by his glorious might."

Waiting for the Lord not only strengthens our "faith muscles" but more importantly, it glorifies God. Here's how it works: our willingness to wait for something or someone reveals the value we place on that *for which* we wait. For a cheap loaf of KwikMart whitebread, I won't brave a ten-minute—or even a one-minute—line. I don't highly value KwikMart bread. But for a loaf of Simple Cafe crusty, chewy, sourdough, I'd gladly wait 10 minutes.

The Civil War bride waited. She didn't accept the proposal because her soldier man was worth it. When we wait for God in his place and at his pace, we show the watching world that He is worth the wait. I don't need to tell you that the injured soldier recovered and was reunited with his ecstatic bride. We love reunion stories. The commercial where the returning soldier walks through the gate then races to hug his Stateside bride makes us cry.

Only the Father knows the date, but a wedding awaits. Bride and Groom, the Church and Christ, *will* be united.

> *Let us rejoice and exult and give him the glory; for the marriage of the*
> *Lamb has come, and his Bride has made herself ready; it was granted*
> *her to clothe herself with fine linen, bright and pure"—for the fine linen*
> *is the righteous acts of the saints.* (Revelation 19:7-8)

One day *only* the meek will dwell in the land. Our meek deeds—our forbearing, forgiving and patient waiting, and in all, our trusting that He intends good—are fine linen. These are our beautiful, God-given wedding clothes. "Then all your people will be righteous; they will possess the land forever, the branch of My planting, the work of My hands, that I may be glorified" (Isaiah 60:21). God will be glorified by our patient waiting, confident in his promise that one day the meek will possess the earth.

Until then, we will have as much as is good for us: "as much as will serve to bear [us] through this world to a better."[17] Who could want more? His grace is sufficient. Enough is as good as a feast.

The valley is the portal through which the meek enter to inherit the earth. In the last chapter we glimpse that final gateway, down in the valley of the shadow.

FOR FURTHER REFLECTION

1. Coming into this chapter, how would you have explained the promise Christ gave to the meek (Matthew 5:5), that they *will inherit the earth?* How has your understanding grown?

2. List and describe three ways that the meek inherit this *present* earth. Which have you experienced recently? Which one do you think requires the most spiritual strength? Why?

3. Reread 2 Peter 1:3-4. How does Peter connect divine promises and power to our ability to live meek and godly lives? Discuss: "The source of our spiritual strength is divine power, and the activating connection between the goal of meekness—and all aspects of godliness—and divine power is knowing and trusting the promises of God."

4. How can these promises empower our meekness? Are there others in the Bible that help you be more meek?

- Matthew 5:5

- 1 Corinthians 3:21

- Psalm 34:10

- Romans 8:32

5. What is the relationship between contentment and "inheriting the present earth"? What do you think Matthew Henry meant by, "Enough is as good as a feast"?

6. Derek Kidner said that the meek "are those who take the way of patient faith over self-assertion." Have you ever thought of the meek as "patient waiters"? Do you agree that "impatient people are weak and therefore dependent on external support—like schedules that go just right and circumstances that support their fragile hearts"?

7. Our willingness to wait for something or someone reveals the value we place on that for which we wait. How does this statement relate to Psalm 39:7?

PRAYER OF RESPONSE

Father of Jesus, please help me to be a patient waiter. "Teach me the happy art of attending to the things of earth with a mind intent on heaven. Help me to walk as Jesus walked, his meekness my clothes. Let my happy place be amongst the poor in spirit, my delight in the gentle ranks of the meek. Let me always esteem others better than myself, and find true humility an heirdom to two worlds."[16] For the glory of Christ,

Amen.

DIGGING DEEPER III

Mighty, Meek Grandma Inherits the Land

> The more your affections are set on Christ, your true husband ... the easier it will be to take you out of the world. He who has laid up his heart in heaven, will think comfortably of laying down his head on earth.
>
> —*George Swinnock*[1]
>
> They were desiring a better country, that is a heavenly one. Therefore God is not ashamed to be called their God, for he has prepared for them a city.
>
> —*Hebrews 11:16*

Your grandma is ready to go home. That was what Grandma said when we asked if she had any last words. Jim and I and the boys had dropped in this one last time. As we said our *good-byes*, Grandma wanted us to know *she* was comfortable laying down her head, comfortable saying good-bye.

The Grandma who so loved life—whose eyes still lit up that last July at the sight of the first purple plums the boys plucked, whose unbroken good humor split open my solemn heaven-talk—*You'll beat me there, Grandma, but I'll meet you.*

Well, then, drive home safely, dear, she breathed, bright-eyed, in her hospital bed. Grandma was ready to lay down her head and go home.

THE FIGHT OF HER LIFE

Back in May the battle bugle sounded. From then on, Grandma fought the fight of her life. Her final war with wince-creating, nauseating, gut-wrenching pain. But her real war was not mainly against pain. The fight would be a spiritual war against darkness and doubt and despair.

This is how the meek fight the good fight of faith. When Grandma started her life's final war, it was with pain. When she learned that the cancer was inoperable and terminal, her soldier prayers were two:

> *Pray that I won't despair and believe Satan's lies. Pray that I will glorify God.*

The enemy did attack Grandma. The fiery darts came in dreadful, discouraging dreams at first. Nightmares of a heaven that is no heaven, and of horrific, not beatific reunions. But Grandma fought back and honored her Lord. Divine power comes through divine promises and Grandma claimed them. "He will wipe away every tear from their eyes, and death shall be no more, neither shall there be mourning nor crying nor pain anymore" (Revelation 21:4). She wielded that sword of the Word with prayer.

The month before she won the war, I spent a night with Grandma. The maple floor under her hospital bed was holy ground, a holy *battle* ground. Because Satan's guns seem biggest in the valley of the shadow of death. When the Victor is coming over the hill and his time is short, he rages hardest. That was this hour on the floor.

But even in that hour, the saints are not in enemy hands, nor even in our own hands. The meek are shaped and turned and, always, held in the best hands. Charles Spurgeon explains[3],

I set my heart and mind on things above and dream of the day I'll see my Bridegroom; I remember the promise of a new body, a new heart and mind. And I think about the crowns I'll be able to cast at Jesus' feet. These things make up the soon and coming reality, so today, get your mind on the hereafter. The soul that mounts up to heaven's kingdom cannot fail to triumph.

—Joni Eareckson Tada[2]

We are under the skillful operation of hands which make nothing in vain. The close of life is not decided by the sharp knife of fate; but by the hand of love. We shall not die before our time, neither shall we be forgotten and left upon the stage too long.

OUR TIMES ARE IN *HIS* HANDS.

But while we'd like to think dying is graceful and painless, and that meek saints fade painlessly into glory, that's not always true. Maybe sometimes departures are that way. But based on Apostle Paul's words and the saintly examples I've seen, it's not the norm. Paul calls all of life, up to and including the end of life, a *fight of faith*. Never does he compare the Christian life to a glide or coast. It is effortful. *Fight of faith, wrestle against powers, run the race* (1 Timothy 6:12, Ephesians 6:12, Hebrews 12:1). Meek saints who rest in God also strive until they die (Hebrews 4:11).

"Pain hurts," Grandma sighed. Choking down anti-nausea pills and retching them back up is horrid. Dying is not without a fight.

"Help me, dear Jesus," she moaned, gagging again, mouth agape over the empty ice-cream bucket.

Dying is spiritually grueling. *Anxiety gnaws like a fire and loneliness spreads out like a desert*, C.S. Lewis wrote[4]. Paul's last days were a fight too. He was deep in the eleventh or twelfth round when in that last letter he wrote, "I've fought the good fight. I have finished the race. I have kept the faith" (2 Timothy 4:7-8).

We meek want to live in such a way that we can claim those stout words for ourselves. Which means we really ought to taste the price that Paul paid to say them. We saw in Chapter 9 that Paul was in chains in a cold prison cell with no hope for earthly deliverance when he wrote them. Scholars think those fighting, triumphant words came weeks or months before his martyrdom at Nero's hands.

In that waiting place, meek Paul wanted his books and parchments. Meek Grandma wanted her books, too. Heaping piles lined her bedside. But one book, *that* Book, was the only book on the caregiver's chair.

After a restless night, awake again before the sun, Grandma was ready for that Book.

"Is Romans 8 okay?" I asked.

Grandma nodded. Then I reached for her hand, and began, "There is therefore now no condemnation for those who are in Christ Jesus."

I squeezed her hand, "For I consider that the sufferings of this present time are not worth comparing with the glory that is to be revealed to us…"

And then, miracle of miracles, the thick tongue whose muffled words I could barely understand moments ago, recited clear and strong,

> *Who shall separate us from the love of Christ? Shall tribulation, or distress, or persecution, or famine, or nakedness, or danger, or sword?*

By dawn's early light, I witnessed another mighty meek miracle I'm sure I will never forget. That frail hand I'd held and rubbed last night, then nestled under the covers; that same hand was exultant—raised high. Pale in her hospital bed, Grandma wielded her sword and finished the chapter with me, "For I am sure that neither death nor life…nor height nor depth, nor anything else in all creation, will be able to separate us from the love of God in Christ Jesus our Lord."

> *Not worth comparing. No condemnation. Nothing can separate.*

Yes, yes, and—hallelujah!—yes.

HEAPING GLORY

But Satan is wily. Even the strongest saints get weary. Predators hunting gazelle try to isolate their prey. Satan takes that tack. He tries to pick off God's weak and weary sheep, alone, away from the flock. But Church, we are a flock and an army. We fight the good fight *together*. We spur each other forward, and lift up drooping arms. Our Captain in the good fight is also our Shepherd in the dark valley. Immanuel, God with us.

Thankfully, Grandma knew that. I heard her murmur, over and over, in the wee hours that night,

> *I will fear no evil. Jesus is with me. I will not fear. He loves me.*

The meek know that while cancer might kill the body it cannot destroy the soul. Grandma knew that pancreatic cancer would be the death of her flesh. The hospital bed and catheter, the water swabs and strong pain meds made that clear. Yes, dying of cancer was the fight of Grandma's life. But it was never a fight *for* her life. Because many decades before doctors diagnosed cancer, her strong, meek life was hidden with Christ in God.

Yes, Grandma, you are heaping glory to God. Your meekness shines brilliantly on your Lord Jesus Christ. Because Grandma knew the Resurrection and the Life. She knows that "whoever believes in me, though he dies, yet shall he live, and everyone who lives and believes in me shall never die." Grandma believed in Him, and made war on fear with that promise, that truth.

Your Grandma is ready to go home.

I thought those were Grandma's last words for us. But there were more. Because after she said that, when the gentle and ginger great-grandma hugs were done, she looked her grandsons in the eyes and oh-so-meekly blessed them,

Boys, if you've got Jesus, you've got everything.

AFTERWARD

In her living and in her dying, Grandma showed me that meekness does not have to fade in even the darkest valley. It can shine brighter. God is up to something good in us, with us, and in all who keep company with us in the valley.

His power and strength, his taming, conforming, comforting grace is with us in the valley. The Good Shepherd is with us. His grace will be sufficient for me. His power will be made perfect in my weakness.

That means that we can expect blessings in the valley. Pastor Kevin DeYoung writes[5]:

> *We all want the mountaintops. The view is great. Exhilarating. But the water always runs down to the valley. Grace always flows down.*

As I type this, it's the month before this book goes to print. I am walking through a shadowy new valley while I write. A diagnosis is coming. I don't know if it will be *the* valley, but I know God is with me. As I await surgery and pathology results to determine the source of my pain, these meek truths are flashing through my mind. I'm trusting grace to flow down the mountain I face. I'm expecting a blessing. Because the doctors said it could be cancer of a particularly lethal variety. It's not likely, but the doctor's "could be" got my attention. Suddenly, I *feel* in myself what I saw in my grandma. I realize that a meek, sit-loose mindset is at its zenith after the dash. By that I mean, in kindness and love, that God has already determined the date of my death.

If meekness is our "attitude of humility toward God and gentleness toward people flowing from trust that God is loving and in control," it is put to the test when God numbers our days with a number lower than we would choose. I won't lie. There are moments when the thought of a life so shortened that I can't see the boys graduate makes me sad. But then the meek-making truths flood my mind, and help me rest.

My times are in His hands. He is good and does good. He gives and takes away. Blessed be His name. All the paths of the LORD are steadfast love and faithfulness, for those who keep his covenant. No good thing does he withhold. The meek will inherit the earth. Nothing, neither death nor life, can ever separate me from the love of God that is Christ Jesus my Lord.

Nothing.

Oh friends, our Lord Jesus Christ is with us in the valley, if we have come to him and taken his yoke—his kind, easy yoke. He says "learn from me, for I am meek and humble of heart; and you will find rest for yourselves. For my yoke is easy, and my burden light" (Matthew 11:29b-30, New American Bible).

The word translated "easy" in "my yoke is easy" has a depth not apparent on the surface. Because even when we go to Christ and learn meekness, our lives don't always feel easy. The end of Grandma's life was the furthest thing from easy. The word translated as "easy" is the Greek word *chrēstos*. It is translated "kind" in Ephesians 4:32: "Be kind to one another, tenderhearted" (also Romans 2:4). It means mild and pleasant.

In the words of Dane Ortlund[6], author of *Gentle and Lowly,*

What helium does for a balloon, Jesus's kind yoke does to his followers. We are buoyed along in life by his endless gentleness [meekness] and supremely accessible lowliness. He doesn't simply meet us at our place of need: he lives in our place of need. He never tires of sweeping us into his tender embrace. It is his very heart.

Sharing the yoke means going through the valley of the shadow with Jesus.

But it's still a valley. With, beside, and in Christ—delighting to do the Father's will—we are more than conquerors. The affliction that would shipwreck the faith of some, strengthens us. "So we do not lose heart. Though our outer self is wasting away, our inner self is being renewed day by day" (2 Corinthians 4:16). Satan's tactic backfires. The meek trust Christ and their souls grow stronger (see Psalm 138:3).

It is only as we live in Christ, with Christ, under his kind yoke that we find the joyful, fruitful, peaceful life He calls us to. As Ortlund writes:

[Only] as we drink down the kindness of the heart of Christ will we leave in our wake, everywhere we go, the aroma of heaven, and die one day having startled the world with glimpses of a divine kindness too

great to be boxed in by what we deserve.

He is our present and future inheritance. Yoked with Him our souls find rest.

So will you look to Jesus? He is the meekest man, the strongest man, the Lion and the Lamb. He is the King of meekness. He came to earth to "revive humanity, and to make those men, who had made themselves beasts."[7] He came to save and redeem sinners (1 Timothy 1:15, Titus 2:12-13). He came like us, so that he could become "a merciful and faithful high priest to help us" (Hebrews 2:17). This was God the Father's will. Jesus Christ came to do the Father's will (John 6:38, Hebrews 10:7). In the gentle strength of Christ, through the mighty power of his Spirit, the meek live to do the Father's will.

"Learn much of the Lord Jesus," Robert Murray McCheyne[8] wrote, "For every look at yourself, take ten looks at Christ. He is altogether lovely. Such infinite majesty, and yet such meekness and grace, and all for sinners, even the chief!" Will we learn from Jesus?

The path to joy, the way to peace, and the track to transform our every trial into triumph is in living the gentle strength of meekness. As we pull life's load, yoked beside our meek and mighty Lord Jesus and doing the Father's will, we realize God's good purpose for us. We are conformed into the image of Jesus as we walk step by step together.

Together, into the Land Without Curse.

In the last chapter of the Bible, John describes the land, a *no longer cursed land*. Because the Lion who is a Lamb, the Mighty King of Meekness is there, reigning in that earth.

> *[A]nd his servants will serve him. They will see his face, and his name will be on their foreheads. There will be no more night. They will not need the light of a lamp or the light of the sun, for the Lord God will give them light. And they will reign for ever and ever. (Revelation 22:3-5)*

Oh yes, Jesus is with us in every valley. Beside him, the Lamb who is a Lion, the Good Shepherd who is the Almighty King of Kings, all God's strong, tamed saints walk through. And then one glorious day the meek shall inherit the land.

FOR FURTHER REFLECTION

1. This chapter was emotional to write. Perhaps it evoked memories of your loved ones. Reflecting on those you know, or on the author's own experience with her grandmother, how have you seen meekness reflected in saints fading into glory?

2. "The close of life is not decided by the sharp knife of fate; but by the hand of love. We shall not die before our time, neither shall we be forgotten and left upon the stage too long," C. H. Spurgeon observed. To yield to God's will when his will is to welcome you into your heavenly home sooner than you expected is the penultimate expression of meekness. Do you agree? Why or why not?

3. Hebrews 11:16 says, "They were desiring a better country, that is a heavenly one. Therefore God is not ashamed to be called their God, for he has prepared for them a city." How does this verse connect with the promise that *the meek will inherit the land?*

4. Discuss the role of God's Word and God's people in "Mighty Meek Grandma's" final fight.

5. "But the water always runs down to the valley. Grace always flows down." Kevin DeYoung used that verse in reference to 2 Corinthians 12:7-10. Read that passage. What do you think it means that "water always runs down to the valley?"

6. Reread Matthew 11:28-30. How has your understanding of these verses developed over the course of this book? Specifically, how would you explain to a friend what it means to "share the yoke" with Jesus?

7. Throughout this guide, meekness has been described as *a gentle strength* and *a taming grace*. Now that we've reached the end of this journey, how would you explain those phrases? Can you explain why the meek are *more than conquerors* (Romans 8:37) and how meekness truly transforms our trials into triumph?

LORD, HIGH AND HOLY, MEEK AND LOWLY,

Thou hast brought me to the valley of vision,

where I live in the depths but see thee in the heights;

hemmed in by mountains of sin I behold Thy glory.

Let me learn by paradox

that the way down is the way up,

that to be low is to be high,

that the broken heart is the healed heart,

that the contrite spirit is the rejoicing spirit,

that the repenting soul is the victorious soul,

that to have nothing is to possess all,

that to bear the cross is to wear the crown,

that to give is to receive,

that the valley is the place of vision.

Lord, in the daytime stars can be seen from deepest wells,

and the deeper the wells the brighter thy stars shine;

Let me find Thy light in my darkness,

Thy life in my death,

Thy joy in my sorrow,

Thy grace in my sin,

Thy riches in my poverty

Thy glory in my valley.

—THE VALLEY OF VISION, "The Valley of Vision"[8]

ACKNOWLEDGMENTS

"Give birth already," they said. But meekness needed growing in me. Till I meet Jesus face to face, it still will. But now is the fullness of time. The baby has been born.

Delivering a book is a community project. I would like to acknowledge the massive debt I owe to all my Joyfully Pressing On readers who read the posts and pray for me. Michele Rae and Stephanie, from conception your comments fed me. Friends, most of your names are not listed here, but I thank my God for you by name. Thank you.

To you who eight years ago saw blips of glory when we began our quest around Cathe's dining room table for that unassuming, neglected virtue—thank you. At unsuspecting moments when I burst forth about meekness, you heard me out. When I announced I would write a book about meekness, you raised your eyebrows. But you did not laugh. After seasons of starts and stops and scrapped chapters and arcane titles (*A Taming Grace*, anyone?), still you dared ask, "When can I read your book?"

Now I am talking about you Susanne and Sarah and Robert, and you, Shari and Mary and Myrt, and you Rachel, Mary Jo, Sandra and Jen. When the baby was conceived ten years ago, and sight unseen for seven more, those unshowing years, you were not too abashed to ask, "How is the book coming?"

Here I hesitate and offer this caveat first: any typos you found are mine, all mine, and for them I sincerely beg your pardon. Jan, but for your eagle eye there would be hundreds more.

To my ridiculously responsive, incredibly generous friend Kat, with enormous skill and great warmth you honed, smoothed, and adorned the message. I needed your wise eyes.

Cheryl, Cindy, Rebecca and Kendra, what a gift you gave. You read the whole bloomin thing and assured me that the message was not lost in my words, the baby in the bath. Thank you.

To the Thursday morning Bible study ladies, Terre, Susan, Christin, Sandra, Danielle, and Sue, the way you plowed through my rough and tumble drafts put wind in my sails. We weeded confusing words and confounding quotes together, though I do miss the soft wool-sack.

Linnea, thank you for sharing your exquisite photo of a horse "used to the hand" (p. 75). It is perfectly meek.

To Taryn and Typewriter Creative, thank you for helping me package this "first-place grace" with the precision and elegance it deserves.

To my Hope*Writer friends, thank you for showing me there are different ways to get the message out. Your words matter.

Charissa and Danielle, Mom and Dad, I would not have been able to get the work done without your lavish love, generous boycare, plus the tacos, chocolate chip cookies and farm-fresh veg.

Jim, thank you for your faithfulness and patience when you weren't so sure about this baby. You loosed me to write, kept me honest and made me laugh.

And, to the Lord who providentially guided a man named Matthew Henry to write *The Quest for Meekness* and *Quietness of Spirit* and land in my hands hundreds of years later, thank you.

ABOUT THE AUTHOR

For more soul-strengthening, biblical content, join
me at www.abigailwallace.com.

It would be my delight to sit and chat with your
book club or Bible study.

Please contact me at joyfullypressingon@gmail.com
if you're interested.

I promise to make it lively.

Join the JoyfullyPressingOn Community
On Instagram @AbigailWallace.4
Or on Facebook @Abigail Wallace

WORKS CITED

Ordered chronologically by chapter

Cover Page

1. Maclaren, Alexander. "Psalm 62 - Maclaren's Expositions of Holy Scripture - Bible Commentaries." StudyLight.org, https://www.studylight.org/commentaries/eng/mac/psalms-62.html.

Dear Friend Letter

2. Bennett, Arthur. The Valley of Vision: A Collection of Puritan Prayers and Devotions. Banner of Truth Trust, 1975, Carlisle, PA, "The All-Good," p. 7.

1 - Meekness & Me

1. Tozer, A. W. The Pursuit of God; the Pursuit of Man. Christian Publications, 1993, chapter 9

2. Bridges, Jerry. "Meek and Merciful." The Gospel Coalition, https://www.thegospelcoalition.org/sermon/meek-and-merciful/.

3. Henry, Matthew. The Quest for Meekness and Quietness of Spirit. Wipf & Stock, 2007, p. 128.

4. Wolgemuth, Nancy DeMoss. "Meekness and Trust" podcast. Revive Our Hearts, https://www.reviveourhearts.com/podcast/revive-our-hearts/meekness-trust/.

2 - Meekness Defined

1. Watson, Thomas. The Comforting Rod, https://www.gracegems.org/Watson/comforting_rod.htm.

2. Henry, Matthew. The Quest for Meekness and Quietness of Spirit. Wipf & Stock, 2007, p. 18.

3. Barclay, William. "Barclay's Daily Study Bible," accessed at https://www.studylight.org/commentaries/eng/dsb/matthew-5.html

4. Pink, Arthur W. Exposition of the Sermon on the Mount. Bottom Of The Hill Publis, 2011, p. 23.

5. Mowczko, Marg. "The Greek Word 'Praus' and Meek Warhorses." 27 Aug. 2022, https://margmowczko.com/meek-warhorses-praus/#_ftn11. An indisputable reference to the meek Peloponnesian war horse was next to impossible to pin down, but this article did an excellent job tracking down an ancient Greek source.

6. Wood, D. R. W. New Bible Dictionary. InterVarsity Press, Downers Grove, 1982.

7. John Piper. "Blessed Are the Meek," sermon, Bethlehem Baptist Church, Minneapolis, February 9, 1986.

8. Bridges, Jerry. "Meek and Merciful." The Gospel Coalition, https://www.thegospelcoalition.org/sermon/meek-and-merciful/.

9. Duncan, Ligon. "Matthew: The Citizens of the Kingdom I" sermon, Faith Presbyterian Church, Jackson, April 1, 1997.

10. "Psalms 62 - Maclaren's Expositions of Holy Scripture - Bible Commentaries." StudyLight.org, https://www.studylight.org/commentaries/eng/mac/psalms-62.html.

11. Kidner, Derek. Psalms 1-72. Intervarsity Press, Downers Grove, IL, 2014, p. 168.

12. See (2)

13. Ferguson, Sinclair, et al. "Is Gentleness for Losers?" The Gospel Coalition, https://www.thegospelcoalition.org/sermon/is-gentleness-for-losers/.

14. Mattoon, Rod. Treasures from the Sermon on the Mount. Lincoln Land Baptist Church, 2006.

15. Blanchard, John. "Blueprint for Blessing - 7." SermonAudio, https://www.sermonaudio.com/solo/blanchard/sermons/5230846468/.

16. DeYoung, Kevin. "Congratulations Are in Order." https://kevindeyoung.org/sermon/congratulations-are-in-order/.

17. Challies, Tim. "Forest Fires & Apple Orchards." Tim Challies, 27 Oct. 2021, https://www.challies.com/articles/forest-fires-apple-orchards/.

18. Watson, Thomas. The Comforting Rod, https://www.gracegems.org/Watson/comforting_rod.htm.

3 - Meekness Matters

1. Challies, Tim. "Forest Fires & Apple Orchards." Tim Challies, 27 Oct. 2021, https://www.challies.com/articles/forest-fires-apple-orchards/.

2. Henry, Matthew. The Quest for Meekness and Quietness of Spirit. Wipf & Stock, 2007, p. 144.

3. Tripp, Paul David. "February 22," New Morning Mercies. Crossway Books, Wheaton, IL, 2021.

4. Ferguson, Sinclair, et al. "Is Gentleness for Losers?" The Gospel Coalition, https://www.thegospelcoalition.org/sermon/is-gentleness-for-losers/.

5. See (2)

6. See (2)

7. Piper, John. "The Goodness of God and the Guidance of Sinners." Desiring God, 30 June 2022, https://www.desiringgod.org/messages/the-goodness-of-god-and-the-guidance-of-sinners.

8. Smith, Colin. "Blessed Are the Meek, Part 1." Open the Bible, 10 June 2021, https://openthebible.org/broadcast/blessed-meek-1-weekend/.

9. "Color Me Beautiful, Beauty for Every Season, Cosmetics and Skincare." Color Me Beautiful, https://colormebeautiful.com/.

10. Spurgeon, Charles. "Psalm 149 Bible Commentary." Psalm 149 Bible Commentary - Charles H. Spurgeon's Treasury of David, https://www.christianity.com/bible/commentary/charles-spurgeon/psalm/149.

11. Henry, Matthew. The Quest for Meekness and Quietness of Spirit. Wipf & Stock, 2007, p. 53.

12. Chambers, Oswald. "May 14." My Utmost for His Highest: Selections for the Year, Barbour & Co., Uhlrichsville, OH, 2000.

13. Henry, Matthew. The Quest for Meekness and Quietness of Spirit. Wipf &
    Stock, 2007.

14. Hughey, Sam. "The Reformed Pastor, Richard Baxter: The Reformed
    Reader." The Reformed Pastor, Richard Baxter | The Reformed
    Reader,   http://www.reformedreader.org/rbb/baxter/reformedpastor/
    trpch1s1.htm.

15. Westminster   Shorter   Catechism   Project,   https://www.shortercate-
    chism.com/.

4 - Meekness Rests on Providence

1. Flavel, John. The Mystery of Providence. Banner of Truth Trust, 1962.

2. "My Times Are in Thy Hand." The Spurgeon Center, 17 May
    1891,   https://www.spurgeon.org/resource-library/sermons/
    my-times-are-in-thy-hand/#flipbook/.

3. Tripp, Paul David. "February 22," New Morning Mercies. Crossway Books,
    Wheaton, IL, 2021.

4. See (2)

5. "My Times Are in Your Hands - Part Two - Truth for Life." Archive
    - Truth For Life, https://www.truthforlife.org/resources/sermon/
    my-times-in-your-hands-pt2/#[2].

6. "Fanny Crosby." Christian History | Learn the History of Christianity &
    the Church, Christian History, 8 Aug. 2008, https://www.christianitytoday.
    com/history/people/poets/fanny-crosby.html.

7. Bridges, Jerry. "Meek and Merciful." The Gospel Coalition, https://www.
    thegospelcoalition.org/sermon/meek-and-merciful/.

8. Ferguson, Sinclair, et al. "Is Gentleness for Losers?" The Gospel Coalition,
    https://www.thegospelcoalition.org/sermon/is-gentleness-for-losers/.

9. "Heidelberg Catechism." Westminster Theological Seminary, https://stu-
    dents.wts.edu/resources/creeds/heidelberg.html.

10. See (9), Catechism #28

11. Edward, Jonathan. "Love Disposes Us Meekly to Bear the Injuries Received from Others by Jonathan Edwards (1703-1758)." Love Disposes Us Meekly to Bear the Injuries Received from Others, https://www.biblebb.com/files/edwards/charity4.htm.

12. Henry, Matthew. The Quest for Meekness and Quietness of Spirit. Wipf & Stock, 2007.

13. See (6)

14. Author's private travel notes from 2014.

15. "Psalm 31 Bible Commentary." Psalm 31 Bible Commentary - Charles H. Spurgeon's Treasury of David, https://www.christianity.com/bible/commentary/charles-spurgeon/psalm/31.

16. See (5)

DIGGING DEEPER I: Meek Not Weak: Correcting Meekness Misconceptions

1. Perry, Jackie. Gay Girl, Good God: The Story of Who I Was and Who God Has Always Been, B & H Publishing Group, Nashville, TN, 2018, pp. 114–115.

2. Goodwin, Thomas. The Heart of Christ, Banner of Truth, Edinburgh, 2011, 63.

3. Ferguson, Sinclair B. The Sermon on the Mount: Kingdom Life in a Fallen World. Banner of Truth Trust, Carlisle, PA1997, 21.

4. Lloyd-Jones, David Martyn. Studies in the Sermon on the Mount, Inter-Varsity Press, London, 1960, pp. 68–69.

5. "Blessed Are the Meek." Desiring God, 30 June 2022, https://www.desiringgod.org/messages/blessed-are-the-meek.

6. Thomas Watson: Beatitudes: An Exposition of Matthew 5:1-12 - Christian Classics Ethereal Library, https://www.ccel.org/ccel/watson/beatitudes.xiv.html.

7. Henry, Matthew. The Quest for Meekness and Quietness of Spirit. Wipf & Stock, 2007, p. 102.

8.   See (1)

9.   Piper, John. "Christ: The Lion and the Lamb." Desiring God, 30 June 2022, https://www.desiringgod.org/messages/christ-the-lion-and-the-lamb.

10. "Congratulations Are in Order." Kevin DeYoung, https://kevindeyoung.org/sermon/congratulations-are-in-order/.

11. Moule, Bishop. "Circumstances are the expression of God's will" quoted in Tileston, Mary Wilder. Joy & Strength, Barnes & Noble, New York, 1993, p. 257.

5 - Joseph: Meekness When Mistreated & Forgotten

1.   Ferguson, Sinclair, et al. "Is Gentleness for Losers?" The Gospel Coalition, https://www.thegospelcoalition.org/sermon/is-gentleness-for-losers/.

2.   Spurgeon, Susannah, and Charles Ray. Free Grace and Dying Love: Morning Devotions. Banner of Truth Trust, 2006.

3.   Edwards, Jonathan, and Don Kistler. Charity and Its Fruits, or, Christian Love as Manifested in the Heart and Life, Soli Deo Gloria Publications, Orlando, FL, 2005, pp. 79–80.

4.   From, The Life and Letters of Janet Erskine Stuart, Elliot, Elisabteh. Keep a Quiet Heart: 100 Devotional Readings, Flemming H Revell, S.l., 2022, p. 134.

5.   The "Godsent wave" is attributed, wrongly this source says, to C.H. Spurgeon. "6 Quotes Spurgeon Didn't Say." The Spurgeon Center, 8 Aug. 2017, https://www.spurgeon.org/resource-library/blog-entries/6-quotes-spurgeon-didnt-say/.

6.   Blanchard, John. "Blueprint for Blessing - 7." SermonAudio, https://www.sermonaudio.com/solo/blanchard/sermons/5230846468/.

7.   Henry, Matthew. The Quest for Meekness and Quietness of Spirit. Wipf & Stock, 2007, p. 133.

8.   Piper, John. "Why Did You Dedicate Spectacular Sins to Joseph?" Desiring God, 23 June 2022, https://www.desiringgod.org/interviews/why-did-you-dedicate-spectacular-sins-to-joseph.

6 - Moses: Meekness When Opposed & Told No

1. Henry, Matthew. The Quest for Meekness and Quietness of Spirit. Wipf & Stock, 2007, p. 35.

2. Bunyan, John. Advice to Sufferers - John Bunyan, https://www.biblebb.com/files/bunyan/sufferers.htm.

3. Guzik, David. Enduring Word, 28 Dec. 2021, https://enduringword.com/bible-commentary/numbers-20/.

4. Rayburn, Robert S. Faith Presbyterian Church, 24 May 2021, https://www.faithtacoma.org/numbers/2008-11-09-pm.

5. Piper, John. "Does God Punish Us with Pain When We Sin?" ChurchLeaders, 16 Mar. 2017, https://churchleaders.com/pastors/pastor-articles/300574-god-punish-us-pain-sin.html.

6. Vos, Catherine F., and Radius Marianne Catherine Vos. The Child's Story Bible. Eerdmans, 2003, 103.

7 - David: Meekness When Disciplined & Provoked

1. Watson, Thomas. Beatitudes: An Exposition of Matthew 5:1-12 - Christian Classics Ethereal Library, https://www.ccel.org/ccel/watson/beatitudes.xiv.html.

2. Bunyan, John. "Part II." The Pilgrim's Progress: From This World to That Which Is to Come, Delivered under the Similitude of a Dream, Hendrickson Publishers, Peabody, MA, 2009.

3. Maclaren, Alexander. Expositions of Holy Scripture: Ezekiel, Daniel and the Minor Prophets; and Matthew Chaps. I to VIII - Christian Classics Ethereal Library, https://www.ccel.org/ccel/maclaren/ezek_matt1.iii.xvii.html.

4. See (2)

5. Repath, Alan. The Making of a Man of God: Lessons from the Life of David, Fleming H. Revell, Grand Rapids, MI, 1962, 253.

6. Guzik, David. Enduring Word, Commentary on 2 Samuel 16, 2 August 2022, https://enduringword.com/bible-commentary/2-samuel-16/.

7. Tripp, Paul David. 242. David And Absalom [David 11], Paul Tripp Podcast, 11 Nov. 2021, https://www.paultripp.com/podcast/posts/242-david-and-absalom-david-11.

8. DeYoung, Kevin. Christ Covenant Church, 21 Jan. 2020, https://christ-covenant.org/sermons/how-to-get-a-good-nights-sleep/.

9. Burroughs, Jeremiah. The Rare Jewel of Christian Contentment, Sovereign Grace Publishers, Lafayette, IN, 2012, 10.

8 - Job: Meekness When Bereaved & Confused

1. DeYoung, Kevin. Biggest Story Bible Storybook, Crossway Books, S.l., 2022, 202-205.

2. Seu, Andrée. Won't Let You Go Unless You Bless Me: A Collection of Essays, World & Life Books, Asheville, NC, 2008, 115–116.

3. Risner, Vaneetha. "If I Only Knew Why." Desiring God, 30 June 2022, https://www.desiringgod.org/articles/if-i-only-knew-why.

4. Piper, John. "God Is Always Doing 10,000 Things in Your Life." Desiring God, 30 June 2022, https://www.desiringgod.org/articles/god-is-always-doing-10000-things-in-your-life.

5. Bridges, Jerry. "Meek and Merciful." The Gospel Coalition, https://www.thegospelcoalition.org/sermon/meek-and-merciful/. This is a summary of a statement Bridges makes beginning at 18:53 in this message.

6. Piper, John. "Job: Rebuked in Suffering." Desiring God, 30 June 2022, https://www.desiringgod.org/messages/job-rebuked-in-suffering.

7. See (7)

8. Lewis, C. S. The Problem of Pain, HarperCollins, New York, NY, 2014. Ch. 6.

9. Sproul, R. C. The Reformation Study Bible: English Standard Version, Reformation Trust, Orlando, FL, 2015, p. 926.

10. Nicholson, Martha Snell. "The Thorn." The Gospel Coalition, 1 Feb. 2010, https://www.thegospelcoalition.org/blogs/justin-taylor/the-thorn/.

11. DeYoung, Kevin. Biggest Story Bible Storybook, CROSSWAY BOOKS, Wheaton, IL, 2022. 201.

12. See (1)

9 - Paul: Meekness When Disappointed & Alone

1. Elliot, Elisabeth. Audio message, "Meekness III." Blue Letter Bible Audio, http://blb.sc/003dGK.

2. Boston, Thomas. Crook in the Lot: Living with That Thorn in Your Side. Christian Focus Publications Ltd.

3. See (1)

4. See (2)

5. Bullock, Charles, and Soole, Laura Sophia. Disappointment—His Appointment poem, Home Words for Heart and Hearth, "Home Words" Pub. House, London, 1896. P. 248.

6. Stott, John R.W. "Paul's Final Charge." All Souls, Langham Place : C004 Guard the Gospelhttps://www.allsouls.org/Groups/139477/Sermons/Sundays/C004_Guard_the/C004_Guard_the.aspx.

7. See (6)

8. See (6)

DIGGING DEEPER II: Jesus: Meekness When Insulted & Misunderstood

1. Lewis, C. S. Reflections on the Psalms. Walker, 1985.

2. Henry, Matthew. The Quest for Meekness and Quietness of Spirit. Wipf & Stock, 2007.

3. Chambers, Oswald. "November 10." My Utmost for His Highest: Selections for the Year, Barbour & Co., Uhlrichsville, OH, 2000.

4. Elliot, Elisabeth. Audio message, "Meekness III." Blue Letter Bible Audio, http://blb.sc/003dGK.

5. Blanchard, John. Blueprint for Blessing-7. Sermon Audio, 1 Jan. 1989, sermonaudio.com/sermon/5230846468.

6. Shirer, Priscilla. The Armor of God. LifeWay Press, 2022. Week 2, Day 2

7. See (6)

8. Sproul, R. C. The Reformation Study Bible: English Standard Version, Reformation Trust, Orlando, FL, 2015, p. 1724.

9. C. S. Lewis, Letters to an American Lady, Grand Rapids, 1967, 57.

10. See (2) p. 129.

11. See (2) p. 70.

10 - More Meek Than Before

1. Lewis, C.S. Mere Christianity.1952: Harper Collins: New York. 2001, 189.

2. Peterson, Andrée Seu. "A Choice to Rejoice." World, 18 Mar. 2017.

3. Henry, Marguerite. Misty of Chincoteague, Rand McNally, Chicago, 1947, p. 42.

4. Austen, Jane, and Donald J. Gray. Pride and Prejudice: An Authoritative Text, Backgrounds, Reviews and Essays in Criticism, W.W. Norton, New York, 2001, p. 115.

5. See (2)

6. Ferguson, Sinclair, et al. "Is Gentleness for Losers?" The Gospel Coalition, https://www.thegospelcoalition.org/sermon/is-gentleness-for-losers/.

7. Henry, Matthew. The Quest for Meekness and Quietness of Spirit. Wipf & Stock, 2007, p. 90.

8. See (1)

9. See (1)

11 - Tending to Meekness

1. The eight ways to help meekness grow is adapted from 10 ways discussed in Colin Smith's message:

2. Smith, Colin. "Blessed Are the Meek, Part 2." Open the Bible, 10 June 2021, https://openthebible.org/broadcast/blessed-meek-2-weekend/.

3. Smith, I think, adapted his list from Section V at the end of Matthew Henry's book, The Quest for Meekness and Quietness of Spirit. Wipf & Stock, 2007. (pp.

4. ten Boom, Corrie. Clippings from My Notebook: Writings and Sayings Collected, World Wide Publications, Minneapolis, MN, 1984, p. 85.

5. Mattoon, Rod. Treasures from the Sermon on the Mount. Lincoln Land Baptist Church, 2006.

6. Edwards, Jonathan, and Don Kistler. Charity and Its Fruits, or, Christian Love as Manifested in the Heart and Life, Soli Deo Gloria Publications, Orlando, FL, 2005, pp. 79–80.

7. Vrbicek, Benjamin. "Can You Really Become Unoffendable?" The Gospel Coalition, 29 June, 2016. https://www.thegospelcoalition.org/reviews/unoffendable/

8. Spurgeon, C.H. "Plentiful Refreshment." Faith's Checkbook, "August 29," by C. H. Spurgeon, https://archive.spurgeon.org/fcb/fcb-bod.htm.

9. Henry, Matthew. The Quest for Meekness and Quietness of Spirit. Wipf & Stock, 2007, p. 61.

10. Emlet, Michael R. Saints, Sufferers, and Sinners: Loving Others as God Loves Us, New Growth Press, Greensboro, NC, 2021, pp. Chapter 2.

11. See (6) p. 112.

12. See (6), p. 90.

13. Burroughs, Jeremiah, and Phillip L. Simpson. Contentment, Prosperity, and God's Glory, Reformation Heritage Books, Grand Rapids, MI, 2013, p. 7.

14. See (7)

15. See (6)

16. Wilde, Oscar, and John Cowper Powys. The Soul of a Man under Socialism: And Other Essays. Doubleday, Page & Company, 1923.

17. See (5)

18. Lutzer, Erwin. "Blessed Are The Meek." Printed transcript of Songs in the Night message, The Moody Church, Chicago, IL, 2006.

19. Bennett, Arthur. The Valley of Vision: A Collection of Puritan Prayers and Devotions. Banner of Truth Trust, 1975, "Christian Love," 135.

12 - The Meek Inherit the Land

1. Ryle, J.C. "Matthew 5:1-12." Matthew Chapter 5, https://gracegems.org/Ryle/m05.htm.

2. MacDonald, George. I was unable to locate the source for the "spiritual retina" quotation. However, it is cited in a variety of commentaries including, "Matthew 5:5 Commentary." Precept Austin, https://www.preceptaustin.org/matthew_55.

3. Piper, John. "What Is Meekness?" Desiring God, 30 June 2022, https://www.desiringgod.org/articles/what-is-meekness.

4. Henry, Matthew. The Quest for Meekness and Quietness of Spirit. Wipf & Stock, 2007, p. 67.

5. See (4) p. 59.

6. Spurgeon, C.H. "The Third Beatitude: The Charles Spurgeon Sermon Collection." The Third Beatitude https://www.thekingdomcollective.com/spurgeon/sermon/3065/.

7. See (4) p. 75.

8. Hughes, R. Kent. The Sermon on the Mount: The Message of the Kingdom. Crossway, Wheaton, IL. 2013.

9. See (5)

10. Enger, Leif. Peace like a River. Corsair, New York. 2018.

11. Rigney, Joe. "Envy." Theology Refresh: Podcast for Christian Leaders, 30 June 2022, https://www.desiringgod.org/interviews/envy. The "great leveler" quote attributed to Sayers' is found here.

12. Lewis, C. S. The Great Divorce: A Dream. Collins, 2015.

13. DeYoung, Kevin. "Congratulations Are in Order." https://kevindeyoung.org/sermon/congratulations-are-in-order/.

14. See (5)

15. The Phillips Brooks story is told and retold, without attribution, as here: Bosch, Henry. "Patience." Odb.org, Our Daily Bread, https://odb.org/US/1995/01/24/patience.

16. Piper, John. "The Power for Our Patience." The Power for Our Patience, Desiring God, 30 June 2022, https://www.desiringgod.org/articles/the-power-for-our-patience.

17. See (4)

18. Bennett, Arthur. The Valley of Vision: A Collection of Puritan Prayers and Devotions. Banner of Truth Trust, Carlisle, PA, 1975, "Christlikeness," 134.

DIGGING DEEPER III:
Mighty, Meek Grandma Inherits The Land

1. Swinnock, George, and J. Stephen Yuille. The Fading of the Flesh and the Flourishing of Faith, Reformation Heritage Books, Grand Rapids, MI, 2009, p. 86.

2. Tada, Joni E. "Getting Your Mind on the Hereafter." Joni and Friends International Disability Center, http://registration.joniandfriends.org/radio/1-minute/getting-your-mind-hereafter/. In this short podcast, Joni reads from her book Heaven, Your Real Home.

3. Spurgeon, Charles. "My Times Are in Thy Hand." The Spurgeon Center, 17 May 1891, https://www.spurgeon.org/resource-library/sermons/my-times-are-in-thy-hand/#flipbook/.

4. Lewis, C.S. The Problem of Pain, HarperCollins Publishers, San Francisco, 1940, 83.

5. DeYoung, Kevin. "The Valley of Vision." Christ Covenant Church, 27 May 2022, https://christcovenant.org/sermons/the-valley-of-vision/.

6. Ortlund, Dane C. "His Very Heart." Gentle and Lowly: The Heart of Christ for Sinners and Sufferers, CROSSWAY BOOKS, S.l., 2021, p. 23.

7. Henry, Matthew. The Quest for Meekness and Quietness of Spirit. Wipf & Stock, 2007, p. 110.

8. M'Cheyne, Robert Murray, and Andrew A. Bonar. Memoir and Remains of Robert Murray M'Cheyne, Banner of Truth Trust, Edinburgh, 1973, p. 293.

9. Bennett, Arthur. The Valley of Vision: A Collection of Puritan Prayers and Devotions. Banner of Truth Trust, 1975, xv.